LOW AND SLOW

HOW TO COOK MEAT

NEIL RANKIN

EBURY
PRESS

Contents

Preface

These sections are usually filled with a culinary journey from a chef's childhood, telling tales of family holidays to France or a mother who taught them to bake bread or make fresh pasta from an early age. You imagine a kind of shabby chic, Aga-sponsored dream sequence, where a boy who was raised by pigs and grew up in an organic vegetable patch ends up in a professional kitchen at 15 washing dishes, embarks on his dream career and lives happily ever after. I don't have that kind of story to tell.

I grew up in Edinburgh and studied physics in Salford. I went on to do a few odd jobs as a Sound Engineer and to open my own business at 25. I started my professional cooking really, really late in life after moving to London. A few regrettable decisions and a financial crash forced me to make another career change and I chose, against all the best and reliable advice given to me, to become a chef.

I started training at a Cordon Bleu school and then pushed myself through some of the toughest Michelin-starred kitchens that would let me through the door. Sometimes I was accepted and nurtured, but most of the time I was written off as someone too old to learn new tricks. On the contrary, though, I did learn fast and worked on my own ideas and dishes on my days off (of which there were very few). I started doing supper clubs and a few private events, and even had a blog about cooking science that I have long since deleted because most of the dishes made me cringe. It took six years of working 80+ hour weeks before someone sent me in a truly life-changing direction.

Adam Perry Lang is part of the reason I am who I am today. He changed the way I looked at cooking and gave me the confidence to discover for myself the way things should be cooked. I owe him much more than he knows and I also know he doesn't ever expect me to tell him as much. Adam introduced me to the basics of how meat should be cooked, and over the years I've taken his methods and developed quite a few of my own theories too, some of which he probably disagrees with.

I've cooked a hell of a lot of meat in my time. I've built barbecues by hand to cook 15 goats for thousands of people; smoked thousands of ribs, briskets and chickens, and every piece possible of cows, goats, pigs, lambs and game; and cooked too many steaks on a grill to mention. I've also overcooked thousands of steaks, over-brined turkeys, cured brisket until it turned purple, cried at how many pork shoulders I ruined at once (and had to open a street food cart with them the next day), and cooked whole pigs whilst drunk – then fell asleep on the floor behind a bar. Even whilst writing this book, I managed to overcook a 4kg rib of beef because I was watching *Daredevil* with the volume up too loud at 11pm and missed my high-tech meat alarm. I think the sheer amount of failures I've witnessed, or executed myself, makes me a better judge of how you should and shouldn't cook meat and goes further than my successes to explain why you should be listening to me at all.

I have an unbreakable passion for meat butchery and cookery, and for the animals to have lived a good, happy life. It's essential for me that the restaurants I work in use only meat that has been bred by small, trusted farms. Where we can, we butcher everything on site, then smoke the meat in a traditional smoker over English oak or grill over charcoal on a robata-style grill. My teams have an attention to detail and knowledge of meat cookery that surpasses most starred restaurants I've eaten in. We don't do things the easy way but we also don't make it hard for the sake of it. We make it the hard way because it tastes better and we enjoy working this way.

Cooking with the understanding of *how* to cook is becoming a forgotten art. However, real butchery and meat cookery is going through something of a renaissance right now and I really hope this continues. I also hope that, with this book, I can play a small part in making a positive change.

I can say without a shadow of a doubt that I love what I do. I'm lucky to be where I am today and I still have a huge amount to learn. I have no regrets and the meat smells are still fantastic.

Neil Rankin

Foreword by Adam Perry Lang

The reason you picked up this book might be the same reason why I zeroed in on Neil the week we opened Barbecoa in London. It was 2011 and I'd just acquired a wood-burning tandoor. We bonded over a particular dish, tandoor-charred squid with smashed avocado.

The dish sounds dramatic, and it was, for all the wrong reasons. For the type of service we were running, it was impractical, requiring too much time and attention. The squid strangled the service, frustrating Neil to the point that he was yelling a lot. He could not produce the little bastards fast enough. I was by his side watching him struggle and admiring his commitment to that squid. He stayed focused, positive and intent on conquering the dish – which he couldn't – and this gave me a deep appreciation for Neil.

As we cooked together more frequently it occurred to me that a mark of a great cook – one of the qualities that separates everyday cooks from the great ones – is curiosity. It's not a trait that can be learned. You have it or you don't. Neil has it. (People who bother to read forewords tend to have it too, so congratulations.)

I use the term cook instead of chef in this instance as a compliment. It's an important distinction. By today's standards, you don't have to be a good cook to be a functioning chef. Many chefs are trained primarily as administrators/culinary technicians. Chefs have access to computers that calculate cook cycles and regulate temperatures and other technology that can monitor almost every single aspect of cooking protein. We have latex gloves, vacuum-sealed bags, clipper-tie bags with cook-chill-retherm cycles to bring food back to life. The process aims to eliminate human error. The modern day chef has so much control, it's hard for mistakes to happen. While this type of chef is necessary and a tremendous asset when feeding large numbers of people fast, there can be a massive disconnect between the chef and the meal.

So why have these sterile systems worked their way into small restaurants? I believe it is a direct result of chefs who don't want to cook – chefs who don't trust their cooks to think, feel and touch the food. They want button-pressers with tweezers to churn out the predictable.

Fire-cooking is unavoidably tactile, 'real' cooking and Neil is one of the heroes leading the charge. He eschews sterility and embraces the flame. He is enthusiastic and connected and has the appropriate burns and scars to prove it. Fire is synonymous with passion and passion is essential to next-level cooking.

I'm really looking forward to seeing what else comes from Neil's kitchen, as well as his mind, but for now, I'm just glad he wrote this book.

Foreword by Fay Maschler

The gift of a Challans duck – the species used by La Tour d'Argent in Paris for their canard a la presse – and the proofs of this book coincidentally arrive at my house on the same day. I look up Neil's instructions for roasting a duck, follow them more or less scrupulously and end up with a creature that gratifyingly resembles the photograph on page 100. The method involving the bird having a couple of sleepovers in the fridge fits in well with a busy time of year and a lot of cooking to be done. The theories about poaching, drying out and breaking down the connective tissue in the skin are validated and the meat turns out a pretty pink, even 'sexy looking' as promised.

The difference between Neil and other chefs is not that he comes at the job from a background in science – he is not alone in that – but that the learning is allied to a highly developed sense of enjoyment (tempered with cynicism) and relaxed immersion in the pleasures of the senses. His ultimate meal he tells us here is Béarnaise with steak and chips. Note the order of ingredients.

As restaurant reviewer for the *London Evening Standard* I knowingly first enjoyed Neil's cooking early in 2013 at John Salt pub in Islington. His inspirations, interpretations and culinary raillery are already diverting and delightful. Tropes such as using dripping from long-aged beef for frying chips and the comprehension of how pickles and fermented vegetables benevolently pierce the richness of healthy fats are in evidence.

Later in the same year in his next position as head chef of Smokehouse N1

his fundamental prowess, underpinned as it is by French classical training, let loose on wood fires and smoking coals makes me conjure up in print that turning point in human evolution when *Homo erectus* (man) learned to control fire, thereby revolutionising nourishment and bestowing governance over the dark and its predators. It sounds dramatic – or pretentious if you prefer – but Rankin does harness the elemental in cooking, an approach that he sets at one with concern for responsible animal husbandry.

Meat is a bit of a parlous subject, but choosing it judiciously, cooking it affectionately and not eating it recklessly is germane to this book. Markedly careful instructions – I now feel that at last I know how successfully to fashion a burger and cook a steak (minute steaks from frozen!) – mean that its exclusion from the diet is unthinkable.

Chefs often write cookbooks which, with long lists of ingredients and recondite methods are out of touch with domesticity but, as shown in this book, professional cheffy practises that arise from the strictures of not being able to cook to an order from scratch can benefit the amateur cook who can chop up a task to suit a crowded day or couple of days. Meat hates to be overcooked, says Neil, so low and slow is the way to go which obviates brining, resting, letting joints come to room temperature and other shibboleths learned at our mothers' knee.

There is a great deal useful and inspiring to be absorbed here from a battle-scarred Scotsman in a trucker's cap with strong tattooed arms, an amused sardonic smile and tongs as the extension of his fingers.

Introduction

In this book, we'll cover cooking techniques for meat that take 15 minutes, up to those needing 10 hours or even several days. Methods may vary slightly but all the recipes work to the same principles. We'll cover steaks, roasts, braises and barbecue. You can recreate all of them in your own kitchen as long as you have an oven and a frying pan, plus a standard BBQ with a hood and a thermometer (although most of the BBQ meats could instead be cooked in the oven, using the same temperatures and times, if you prefer).

This book is intended for everybody – not just people with expensive grills and barbecue equipment. *It's about the process of cooking meat, not the equipment.*

I've tried to distil all the scientific stuff to give you the essential gist. You don't really need to know the detail. I am quite geeky when it comes to science and meat, though, so I apologise if I veer off track now and again.

The most important thing about this book is that, whilst I am attempting to fast-track you through the years of experience I've needed to develop a feel for cooking meat, I know it's never going to be entirely possible.

There are so many wild variables in cooking meat that may cause these recipes to not go 100 per cent right first time. But that's real cooking.

Hopefully, with this book it won't take you as long to catch up.

The other factor to take into consideration is that all of this is only my opinion. There are many ways to cook a piece of meat. If you're the kind of person who's stuck in his ways, then this book is not for you. There are things chefs have taught me that will stick with me for life, but there are also things great chefs have taught me that I've discounted. Even during the writing of this book, I've changed some theories I've held on to for years because *it's the result that's important, not the method.*

Most of the time, chefs and cooks learn from what we are taught and told, but a lot of old-school theories and rules should be tested to the limit to check they still hold true. Without doubt, the yes-chef-no-chef mentality has led to a huge wave of Chinese-whisper theories that have left many of us without the skills to cook food the way it should be cooked. Thank god for people like Harold McGee, who has shown us how wrong we are.

As a chef I did what I was told, but as a scientist I also always questioned why we did things in a certain way. This book is my answer to my own many questions. Try to have an open mind but also try to have your own opinions too.

Many of these recipes are convenient to make in an evening, whilst some are hobbies to have a go at on a free weekend. The link between all the recipes here is that they follow the methods I use to cook meat perfectly time and time again.

Please let me know how you get on, good or bad. I'd love to find out.

What is low and slow?

Slow cooking at low temperatures is like playing tennis with a bigger racket, a smaller net and a bigger court. It's possibly more tiring and it definitely takes a little longer but the chances of hitting that ball over the net are much greater.

Most importantly, the chances of failure are reduced immeasurably.

In general, we cook everything way too high most of the time. We cook for convenience rather than for what's appropriate to the meat. Low-and-slow cooking is about understanding meat and what's good for it. It's about treating it with respect. It's about cooking the way we were meant to cook and not for convenience and speed.

The irony is that convenience is largely a restaurant restraint when chefs have customers to serve who demand their food to be ready on time. It's my belief that it's easier to get better results at home because you don't have the same time pressures. I've heard a few people say they cooked a better rib at home than the one they ate in my place. This may or may not be true, but try cooking 100–200 ribs every day of the week and serving them perfect over a 6-hour period, as well as cooking 15 other dishes. It's more challenging.

When we cook in a 200°C oven, we might have a 10-minute window for when we should take the dish out (because it cooks faster and will continue to cook after we bring it out), but when we cook the same dish at 100°C we have maybe about an hour's window. When we lower the temperature, we increase the time needed to cook the meat. We also increase the timeline for when it's ready and lose less moisture during cooking (unless we cook too low and we hit a 'stall'; see page 186).

People may think low and slow is just Texas-style BBQ or stews and braises. But in this book I hope to convince you that any meat can benefit from slow cooking – or at least a form of slow cooking, from steaks and chops to roasts and even pies.

Low-and-slow is not even restricted to meat, but that's another book entirely.

How to cook meat

These three rules apply to all meat cookery, from steaks to barbecues and roasting large joints.

RULE 1: COLOUR, COLOUR, COLOUR…

…and colour some more. When I say colour I mean a shade of brown and not a shade of black. Black marks taste bitter. A burned flavour can have positive effects – with scorched vegetables, fruit, lamb and chicken to some degree, and heavily marinated meats also – but as a rule burning should be avoided where possible and on beef especially so.

Brown colour is gained from applying a medium–high heat (140–160°C) to the meat, which at a certain temperature and moisture level creates something called the Maillard reaction. This is the holy grail of meat cooking, the g-spot and the hole in one. When we think of eating meat, the flavours we imagine mostly come from this process. I could bore you at this point by talking in depth about amino acids and non-enzymatic browning and all that other scientific stuff, but I won't.

Instead, I'll say that you should think of this colour as a seasoning – a magic seasoning that unlike salt has no limits to how much you can apply. This is most crucial when cooking steak (see page 34).

In this book, we will refer to this process as searing as it's a commonly used and understood term. Colouring is a better description of what we're trying to do, however. For more on when to brown meat, turn to page 19.

RULE 2: TEMPER, TEMPER, TEMPER

To me, tempering is the essence of meat cooking. It's the way to guide meat to a perfect internal cooking temperature that is as evenly distributed as possible, using whatever medium you have at your disposal. It could be an oven, a poaching liquid, a smoker, warm room or the heat already in the meat. It doesn't really matter because the desired result is always the same. If you want to cook meat perfectly inside, or as perfectly as you can – whether rare, medium or cooked until it almost falls apart – tempering is the method to use to bring the meat to that point.

The temperature you may wish to bring it to varies mostly according to how much connective tissue and fat there is within the meat. For example, a shin of beef, which has lots of tissue, needs long, slow cooking at a reasonably high heat to melt the collagen before it has a good texture. A good fillet steak, however, needs no cooking at all in most cases. This is because a fillet has never done a hard day's work in its life. It just sits there chilling out with no moving parts, so it has less internal fat and collagen than any other meat on the carcass.

Most of this book is about how to follow these first two rules. Usually this means cooking both directly (close to the heat source) for colour and indirectly (not in direct contact with the heat source) for tempering, but sometimes this is not the case. For instance, given enough time we can cook anything far away from the heat source and still develop colour. This is best demonstrated in the South American-style whole-animal cooking where a lamb or pig is hung up near, but not close to, an open burning fire. The size of the animal dictates the long cooking time and therefore the heat needs to be gentle, but the end effect is the same. The Maillard reaction is most effective at 140–160°C, but it can be achieved at lower temperatures if time at that temperature is increased.

To summarise, tempering is cooking but is more than just cooking. To cook something is too unspecific – it's just A to B. Tempering is about breaking it down a bit further and looking at it with an eye for what works best rather than what will just do, so the meat or whatever isn't raw any more.

RULE 3: SEASON, SEASON, SEASON

If the meat is good quality and you've followed the first two rules above, the only thing to stop a piece of meat from tasting great is seasoning. This can mean simple salting or brining, curing or a complex rub. You could even baste the meat with a brining solution or soy sauce during cooking.

Whatever your take is on the health benefits or demerits of salt, seasoning is just as important as the other two rules because without it the meat will still taste of next to nothing, even if we sear it well.

Salt is not only there for flavour. Without salt, our mouths won't produce enough saliva for the meat to seem moist. Most of the moisture we feel when eating a steak can usually be attributed to the salt added. So when someone says 'this is a really juicy steak', what they mean to some degree is 'this is a well-seasoned steak, cooked well'. Obviously, the moisture content of the steak and the cooking play a huge part (a dry steak is a dry steak no matter how much you salt it) but it's largely your saliva you're feeling rather than the juice in the steak. (See page 30 for more on when to season steak.)

Before cooking

Always start cooking meat straight from the fridge (this probably goes against everything you've ever been told). In reality, bringing meat up to room temperature first doesn't really benefit the cooking, and it takes a long time for a large piece of meat to come up to room temperature just by leaving it out of the fridge. During a low-and-slow cooking process at 120°C, warming a 1kg steak to room temperature would take maybe 5 minutes. Even a big steak, such as a 3.8kg rib roast, takes only 20 minutes. In order to bring a 2kg joint or steak to room temperature just by leaving it out on the worktop would take 3–4 hours or more, depending on how warm your room is. I think that's a waste of time. Low and slow is about more efficient cooking.

Now, I'm making a huge assumption that 'fridge-cold' means 8–10°C. I do realise that fridges are supposed to be at 5°C but, in my experience, domestic fridges aren't that great at holding temperature and the core temperature is usually higher than whatever your fridge is cooling to. The door seals are weak and we also open and close the fridge door a lot, so the air temperature inside fluctuates. If you have a super high-tech fridge and your meat is cooler, these times will still work within the parameters.

Meat quality

The treatment of livestock is something I care deeply about. Knowing where your meat comes from is something every chef and butcher should take very seriously.

There are a lot of terms used that suggest good-quality meat – from 'organic', 'free-range', 'grass-fed', 'outdoor-reared' or 'quality-assured' to something attached to a well-known brand name or locality or area that we perceive to be a purveyor of quality meat. In reality though, like the wine industry, most of these terms are pretty meaningless. The only thing that matters to the taste of the meat is the way the animal was treated, how long it has lived and what it was fed.

Whether you're a duck, a chicken, a cow, a pig or a human, the 'you are what you eat' thing is actually science. Like good wine, good meat is a matter of yield. With wine it's all about soil quality, the weather, vitamin and mineral content, and how many vines per acre – the more vines, the less nutrients per grape, hence poorer quality wine. And you can't just grow wine grapes on any piece of land.

With grass-fed meat and other quality feed, it's the same idea: we need a good soil to grow good grass, grain or other feed, to yield great-tasting meat. And we can't overpopulate that grass with too many animals or grow too much grain, otherwise we get fewer nutrients. Quality meat takes time. You can bulk up any animal with high-volume feed and it will develop marbling and a high-fat content. But to develop the high-nutrient content that excellent-tasting meat requires, you need time and the nutrients from quality grain, grass or local vegetation and fruits.

Meat from an old animal fed high-quality nutritious ingredients will always taste better than that from a one-year-old fed on tasteless feed or husks. It may not be as fat, as tender or as marbled, but the flavour will be akin to the difference between a vintage Château Pétrus and a cheap bottle of supermarket Bordeaux.

We know that any stress felt by the animal in the last few hours before slaughter can have a dramatic effect on the quality and taste of the meat, but whether small stresses early on in an animal's life can have any lasting effect on the end product is open to debate. However, if a producer spends time and money rearing livestock on expensive land or using expensive feed, focusing on quality over commerciality, he is unlikely to mistreat his animals. On the farms I visit, they treat their animals almost as well as their own children, in some cases better. This is not a high-profit method of farming. Some producers do it because they want to keep native breeds alive or they have a tradition of farming certain breeds that has been passed down to them through generations. In a vegetarian's eyes, the idea of a caring meat farmer is something of an oxymoron, but if you take the morality of meat-eating out of the equation, there are a lot of producers out there who care deeply about their livestock.

The question is, though, how can we tell the quality of the meat if the labels don't give us the whole story? The answer, unfortunately, is that you can only do this by tasting it. There are visual clues to mistreatment and poor living, especially in pork and poultry, but these can be misleading. Marbling is only really a display of fat content – it doesn't give any indication of flavour, though the distribution of fat and the colour of the meat and fat do give an indicator of age, feed and how slowly the meat was grown to its finishing weight.

In the end, the best way to ensure quality is to buy from farms, butchers, markets or any supplier you trust. But prepare to be disappointed occasionally because no matter how good the producer, the breed or where the meat was produced, there is always the likelihood of it not tasting as good as the last piece.

Whether that is because the animal wasn't as hungry, was a picky eater, was a little depressed for some reason or just didn't want to play ball all its life, it's a fact that animals that haven't been force-fed will have natural variables we can't predict. The animal, it seems, didn't want to taste good and who can blame it?

Rare breeds

Most of the meat available today is the product of a few selective breeds and cross-breeding between them.

The problem with these breeds is that they have been selected largely from a commercial perspective, not for taste. Angus cows, for instance, can grow quickly and produce a good fat content from less feed, which makes them more cost-efficient than other rare breeds whilst being great tasting beef. Dexter cows, in comparison, need more feed to produce a cow about half the size of the Angus. Dexters grow slowly, but if the feed is good, each square inch of flesh develops with a higher intake of nutrients over its lifespan, so the beef tastes more beefy.

Rare-breed pigs have a similar story and generally have a much higher fat content, which unfortunately we tend to shy away from. Our appreciation for meat has gone from being all about the fat, which is what we have naturally craved ever since we learned to hunt, to becoming all about lean flesh. This is purely due to the commercial meat industry and probably driven by consumer concerns over the health issues surrounding fat.

Sadly, if you serve a pork chop with a huge band of fat, people complain, when in fact they should be thanking you for serving more of the best-tasting bit.

Mutton and hogget vs lamb

There are a lot of variances on what defines lamb, hogget and mutton. Most commonly though, lamb is under 12 months old, hogget between 12 and 18 months, and mutton older still at over 2 years.

All you really need to know is which is the oldest and the youngest. The younger lamb will have a more delicate flavour and be tender, whilst the older mutton will be the toughest but with the biggest flavour, given proper feeding and living conditions.

Corn-feeding v grass-feeding

A lot of high-graded American USDA (United States Department of Agriculture) beef and Waygu beef (Waygu is a range of Japanese cattle breeds known for their marbling, but also taken as a common colloquialism for the farming methods used) can be as good, and sometimes better, than grass-fed beef. Europeans get a little snobby about corn-fed beef, but good beef is good beef, full stop.

Opinions on either side of the argument are largely driven by what we've grown up with, and how our tastes have developed, rather than either product being better or worse than the other.

The process of rearing corn/grain-fed cows is all to do with maximising marbling. This does, however, create room for abuse in intensive farming because you can fatten a cow up in haste using cheap grain by-products. Cows can't digest these properly, so they get sick and, in some extreme cases, they then have to be pumped full of chemicals to survive the intense diet. Due to its high commerciality, this rearing method is now found in many countries, including Argentina which used to be known only for its natural grass-fed cattle. Some people see this as a fundamental flaw in corn feeding but this only became a problem when the demand for cheap beef forced the industry in this direction.

The idea of grass-fed animals is all well and good but it's not a consistent process. One herd may produce both great beef and some poor. It uses up a lot of land too and we don't have enough to feed the whole world. So the actual percentage of good grass-fed beef in our production line is pretty small and expensive.

On a personal note, I prefer grass-fed beef to the high-fat marbled stuff. I don't care much for tenderness; it's all about flavour for me. I also like meat from older animals that have lived and moved about – around 2–3 years plus – which may be a little tougher but is very flavoursome.

At a realistic level, a blend of the two is probably more sustainable in the long run, with a little bit of grass and then grain finishing to give a fatter animal without making it sick and without relying on such low yields.

Farming and the environment

The problems with meat production in general is that we eat far too much of it and especially beef. I'm an advocate of meat eating and a big meat eater myself, but we also need to be sensible in our approach when considering the environment. Beef especially should be a luxury. If we eat too much of it not only will we use too much of our land's crops on feeding livestock rather than on feeding starving humans, but we're also more likely to produce a lot of crappy beef.

Calling for a total halt on all meat eating is also a call for wiping out several species of animals, which seems a little rash and selfish too. The problem isn't meat, it's basic greed and whatever we replace meat with we'll end up with similar problems. Let animals live longer, find a more carbon neutral method and eat better meat, less often. If you don't want to do it to save the world, do it because it means better meat.

When to colour meat

One school of thought says that you should cook your meat first at a low temperature, then brown it after (reverse sear) – the idea being that because you have cooked the meat and its surface is drier, the proteins and the browning effect will be quicker and more efficient. This post-browning can be most tricky when applied to cooking small steaks and other small cuts of meat, but can be very effective for large steaks of 1kg plus.

The other school of thought is that you should brown your meat first, then slow-cook it because since your meat is colder to start with you can give it more time at a high heat without overcooking it. This method works for both large and small cuts of meat and, I think, develops a much deeper, thicker crust, which cannot be achieved as well with reverse sear.

Both theories have merit. However, the only times I might post-brown meat is when it has skin and I need an initial slow-cook to render out the fat and break down the collagen (see also Crispy Skin in Roasting, page 90), or if I'm smoking the meat and I need the smoke to penetrate a moist un-crusted outer layer.

If you want more smoke in your meat (only useful when cooking over quality wood) start low and finish high, but if you want a deep rich crust then start high and finish low.

Searing meat

I use pans, griddles or BBQ grill bars to sear most meat, with the exception of birds because of their awkward shape. These give direct-heat cooking, meaning that the heat on their surface transfers to the meat with more efficiency than indirect heat (e.g. inside an oven). The ideal temperature to sear meat is 140–165°C in the pan.

The heat of the gas burner, induction surface or charcoal on a grill is much hotter, but of course heat is lost through the process of heating up the pan and also lost to the air and through the meat.

You don't have to measure this pan temperature; simply use your ears. If the meat makes a loud sizzling noise, the pan heat is doing its job.

If all is quiet, you're wasting your time. Take your meat out of the pan, turn up the heat and leave the pan to heat for a further minute before you put the meat back in.

Why you should move meat around the pan

When you place steak in a hot pan, the heat from the pan is transferred into the meat, meaning the pan temperature around the meat will be higher than that of the pan in contact with/under the meat. By moving the steak around the pan you can continue to cook it on a hotter surface.

Why you should flip meat regularly during cooking

Heat will always be conducted from the hottest parts to the coldest parts of the steak, which is the secret to getting the most perfect cook possible. We not only use the heat in the pan but also the steak's own stored thermal energy.

By flipping meat regularly in the pan, as you can see from the diagram on page 20, you can achieve a constant heating and cooling of the outside core. When we flip a steak, for example, the hottest part of the steak (which was cooking on the surface of the pan before the flip) cools as the heat is transferred to the air and the steak's core. This heating and cooling balancing act means that we can evenly cook the steak despite the high heat of the surface of the steak. If you've ever seen a steak that has a brown overcooked surface and a raw middle, it's likely that this flipping technique was not used, or the grill or pan was too hot.

How meat cooks in an oven

This is the heart of the low-and-slow method of cooking. To understand heat and how it flows, it's helpful to think of it as energy rather than just a number on a dial. The sun is 15,000,000°C, yet when I was growing up in Scotland you could be forgiven for thinking that the sun was powered by a few AA batteries or a mouse running round a wheel.

The energy from the heat source (in this example, the sun), when sent indirectly in all directions, is massively reduced by the time it reaches us. The same thing happens in an oven.

I use a fan oven temperature of 120°C in this book for a very good reason. It might seem logical to think that if your oven is set at 120°C, the outer surface of the meat is cooking at 120°C. In fact, this isn't the case.

As with the sun, the temperature of the air inside the oven is reduced by a number of factors (such as moisture evaporation, energy going to the meat and the oven surfaces leaking heat). The surface temperature of the meat will really be more like 55–60°C (about 50 per cent of the air temperature).

Until the core (or middle) of the meat reaches 50–60°C, the temperature of the surface will not increase above this level. This means the outside should never overcook as long as you don't leave the meat in the oven once the core has reached the desired temperature. You could cook on an even lower temperature, which would lengthen the cooking time, but 120°C will avoid too many mistakes and our time is precious even when cooking low and slow.

The diagrams on the next page (I've done them as circles but this works for most meat shapes) show not only how the meat cooks slowly at 120°C, but also why cooking at a high temperature is not very efficient for browning meat.

Direct cooking in a pan

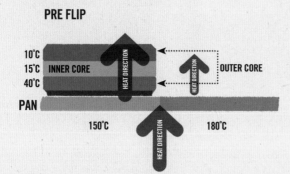

PRE FLIP

10°C
15°C   INNER CORE
40°C

HEAT DIRECTION

OUTER CORE

PAN

150°C   HEAT DIRECTION   180°C

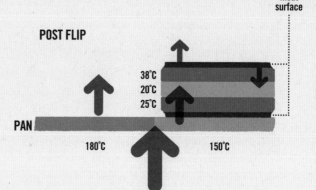

POST FLIP

meat surface

38°C
20°C
25°C

PAN

180°C   150°C

Indirect cooking at high heat

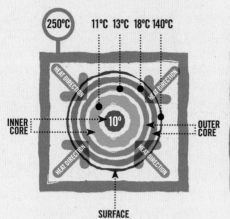

250°C   11°C 13°C 18°C 140°C

HEAT DIRECTION

INNER CORE

10°

OUTER CORE

HEAT DIRECTION

SURFACE

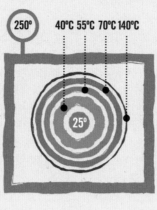

250°   40°C 55°C 70°C 140°C

25°

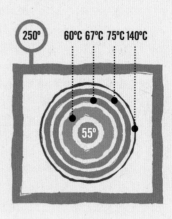

250°   60°C 67°C 75°C 140°C

55°

Indirect cooking at low heat

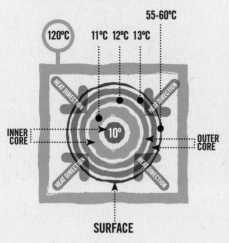

120°C   11°C 12°C 13°C   55-60°C

HEAT DIRECTION

INNER CORE

10°

OUTER CORE

HEAT DIRECTION

SURFACE

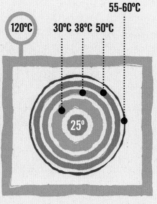

120°C   30°C 38°C 50°C   55-60°C

25°

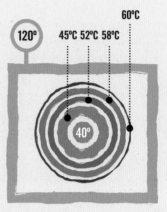

120°   45°C 52°C 58°C   60°C

40°

T I M E

Using higher temperatures

A 220–250°C oven will only create a meat surface temperature of roughly 110–125°C if the meat is cold inside. The meat will colour over time but it will take far longer than if you are cooking under direct heat, and you risk an overcooked outer core as greater time is spent at this temperature.

A 350°C plus oven may sound sexy, but science would prove this temperature to be over-kill and actually damaging to our enjoyment of the meat, unless only used for short periods of time.

At a surface temperature above 165°C, we move past the glorious Maillard reaction to caramelisation. This uses up the sugars and therefore inhibits the Maillard reaction, becoming what we refer to in the trade as 'burning the crap out of something'.

Another thing to consider is why it's bad to cook meat at even medium-high temperatures for any lengthy period of time. Temperatures such as 160°C or 180°C will create a surface temperature of 80–90°C and an outer core temperature of 70–80°C after a short time period, so the outer core is well-done very soon into the cook.

Reheating meat

Reheating meat has a bad rep. This is because, generally speaking, meat is not reheated to make it better but to make cooking/serving it more convenient. It is the calling card of many a lazy, corner-cutting chef. It's also considered a health risk, although it's only a risk with bad temperature control. Fundamentally, though, meat that has been heated and cooled, then reheated properly is just as good or even better than the stuff that comes straight off the grill. You just have to do it right…

1. Cook meat at a low temperature slowly so that it cooks evenly and reaches a safe internal temperature. Chill the cooked meat in under an hour or as efficiently as possible.
2. As when you cool anything, some (but by no means all) of the moisture on its way to being pushed out during the cooking process penetrates back into the meat. If you've added salt to the meat, this happens even more easily on the surface too. Pulled cooked meat cooled in its own juices tenderises over time, and the longer you leave it, the better it gets.
3. Any crust can be re-formed. To reheat, cook the meat at a high temperature – generally in the region of 200–250°C – and quickly to give it lots of colour. You don't need it to reach the same safe internal temperature as when it was cooked from raw, so it won't end up overcooked and dried out. This whole theory is perfectly safe if followed correctly. Also it opens up many more avenues for new cooking methods and convenient home cooking.

Equipment

It would be disingenuous for me to say it doesn't matter what equipment you use but there is some truth in it. As long as your pans haven't been run over by a truck and your oven actually works, you should be fine to cook almost anything. Most professional kitchens use horribly damaged equipment and serve hundreds of people with it. Most of the time your success is really down to technique. That said, a few extra pieces of kit can help:

1. A FOOD PROBE THERMOMETER

The more expensive ones (£30 and above) are usually better as they will read the temperature faster, meaning you don't have to stop the cooking for a long time to check where it's at. But any thermometer, as long as it's not out of a cracker, will be more beneficial than none.

Food probes give us information we can rely on – information that is impossible to get otherwise. If you think chefs can tell when a joint is done using sight or touch, you're wrong. We're not Jedis. Most probe and those who don't usually have haphazard results or cook the same thing day after day and know via repetition.

When you get your probe, check it reads 0°C in melting ice water and 100°C in boiling water. Then you're ready to go.

That 'touch the cooked meat and it feels like your hand' crap is massively inaccurate. It doesn't take into account ageing, bone-in, different cuts, heavy crusts or steaks after cooling. Buy a probe thermometer and it will save you years of pain.

2. AN OVEN THERMOMETER

One of these can cost less than a pound and will prevent your oven from getting away with murder. Fact is, your oven lies – not all the time and not all ovens, but unless it is a super high-spec oven from the future it has flaws. We rely on one thing when slow-cooking and that's cooking temperature.

If you're cooking for hours and hours you really want to know that your oven is as hot as it says it is.

Once again, check your thermometer in melting ice water and boiling water regularly (as before).

3. BUTCHER'S STRING

Have a roll to hand or get those pre-made butcher's string loops from a catering store. Then you don't need to be good at knots. It's always helpful when you're cooking something for it to be an even shape. Not all meat is, so string does come in handy.

4. CAST-IRON PANS AND GRIDDLES

Cast iron is the nuts. Some say it heats evenly but in my experience it actually heats pretty unevenly. What it does do, however, is hold heat like nothing else. In high-temperature searing, that's your golden ticket. With a normal steel pan, when the heat transfers into the meat there is a sharp drop in temperature as energy is lost and it takes time to recover, meaning the heat directly beneath your steak will be the coldest part of the pan. So you have to move the steak around a lot (see diagram on page 20). The same goes for cast iron but the heat drop-off is much less, meaning you can cook faster and sear harder even at lower temperatures. Ridged griddles are also good for meats that have less than even surfaces. You can pick up a cast iron pan for under £15 and it will last you a lifetime. Many cooks are put off by tales of not being able to wash cast iron and having to season it every day. In fact, you can wash it like a normal pan, though dishwashers are not advised, and you shouldn't leave it in water for a long time. Season it now and again by heating it up and rubbing it with a little vegetable oil using a cloth, then let it cool down. It will last forever unlike your non-stick pan, which has a very short lifespan if you use it more than twice a week.

5. TONGS

These are to a meat cook what a knife is to a butcher or a sword to a ninja. Tongs are an extension of your arm and you have to work with them all the time. I never go anywhere without a spare pair. Get the all-metal ones and make sure they are at least 25cm long. You will use them all the time in lifting your meat, hot and cold, and moving it around to check the sear.

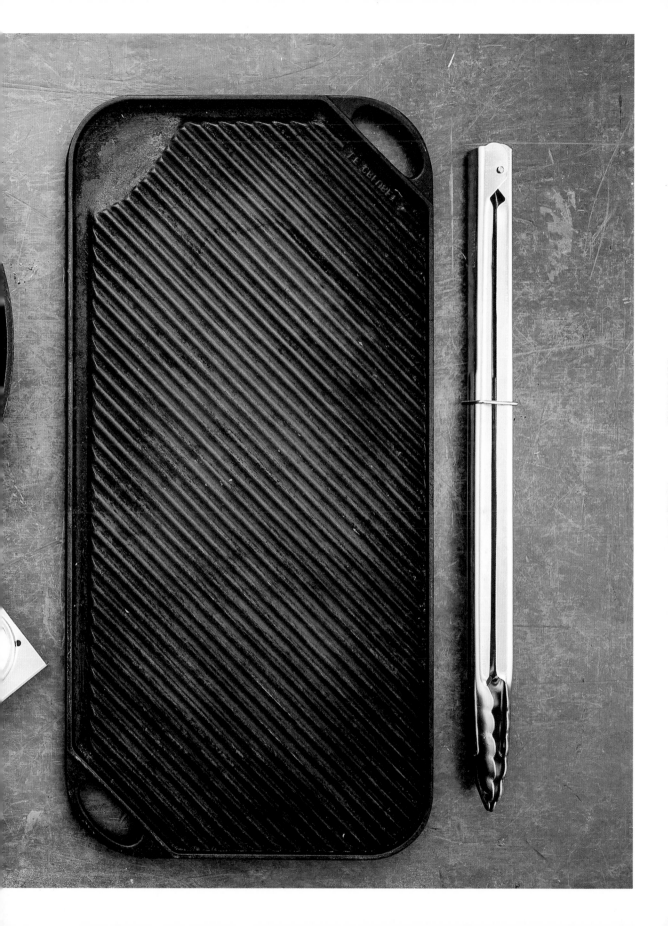

STEAK

There is very little in life as disappointing as a bad steak. In my all-time top ten list of let-downs, it ranks up there with teenage sex, New Year's Eve parties and my golf game. That said, I can remember the first time I had sex and played golf, but I can't for the life of me remember the first bad steak I had. The first *great* steak I had was not until I was 29, and this I can remember to the hour and day. It was in Ibiza and I had already drunk enough wine to kill a horse, which makes it all the more remarkable. But I can still taste the subtle ageing notes, perfect seasoning and umami-rich crust when I think about it today. Since then I've cooked nearly 32,000 steaks and eaten – or at least nibbled on – more than half of those.

It was probably around steak number 10,000 that I began to gain an understanding of why I'd had so many bad steaks, and probably at 20,000 that I started to develop a usable theory for cooking them. In short, I've cooked a hell of a lot of bad steaks myself. The difference is I now know how to spot one. The reason I started this book with a chapter on steak is not only because it's what most of us cook when we think of cooking meat, but also because I believe the three fundamental principles that you need to follow to cook a perfect steak are the same as for cooking all meat. So if you can master them with steak, you can cook anything.

Bashing out steaks

Steak cooking is all about surface area and crust development.

By bashing a thick steak, to make surface area that can form the crust larger, the flavour will be enhanced immensely. You can use almost anything to do the bashing but I would suggest using something flat and heavy, like a strong frying pan or saucepan. When I say bashing out, we're not talking pancake-flat, just reducing the thickness by around 50 per cent, and this is only usually appropriate for thicker steaks.

The reduction in a steak's thickness also means it takes less time for heat to permeate the core, so you can develop a better temperature ratio inside the meat.

Great-tasting meat is not about flat surfaces and boring symmetry. It's about texture and interest in every bite. This is why Adam Perry Lang added roughing-up to the bashing-out process, using a knife or sharp implement. This roughing-up (or scraping) creates even more surface area. The reasoning is similar to that of roughing-up potatoes before roasting them. This increases the usable surface area for browning. The easiest way to do this is to give the steak a few shallow cross slashes with a sharp knife or another sharp implement.

Rough up your meat a little and see what happens. I promise it almost never fights back and tastes delicious.

Bone or no bone?

Does a bone add to the flavour of a steak? No. Does it get in the way of how well you cook a steak? Yes.

Let's face it, bones are a way for restaurants to sell you less meat for more

money, and they look cool. In reality, you're far better off chopping them off and cooking them separately or feeding them to your dog. I love chewing on a good bone with a steak, but I prefer a perfectly cooked steak with a good crust all over. Bones prevent us from getting good surface area cooking and minimise the cooking surface. Plus they conduct heat at a different speed to the meat, meaning it's harder to get an even cook.

Colouring steak/searing

You can't over-colour a steak. You can layer colour upon colour upon colour until it's so dark it almost looks black. The more you add, the more delicious the steak will become.

Called the Maillard reaction, this is the same process that gives the flavour to coffee, toast, bread, roast potatoes, malt whisky and beer. Imagine a coffee without that roasted tone from the beans and now compare that to what you'd be missing out on with a pale steak. It's the same tragedy.

With that in mind, please throw out the idea of cross-hatching meat with grill or griddle marks. That criss-cross pattern we like to put on steaks to show off does not have enough flavour impact. It colours less than half of the steak. Let me put it this way: would you ever butter your toast in criss-cross lines? No, you spread your butter all over.

If you want to put a design on something then learn how to draw or paint. You want to be a good steak cook, then colour and flavour your steak as much as you can.

Seasoning steak

You can season your steak at any point, but the best times are well ahead of cooking it, just before it goes into the pan or during the cooking.

The reason I suggest well ahead is mainly to do with moisture. When we salt something it extracts moisture, which will harm our ability to colour the steak because we need it to be dry to do this. Pre-salting is like curing – it's great but we need to allow time for the salt to draw out the moisture and then more time for that moisture to dry
(1 hour plus for me).

I prefer to season meat in the pan, waiting until the steak is hot enough for the salt to dissolve over its surface, because otherwise it just burns or gets rubbed off. In a restaurant, I usually pre-season, before I cook, but that's only because I may forget to do it later on if I'm busy and have a lot of steaks on the grill. Use fine salt – you can simply blitz Maldon sea salt in a blender or, if you can get it, use American

kosher salt. Coarse salt may look sexy but when pan-frying it clumps together and burns easily.

Let's lay 'resting' to rest

I've never understood what resting means and I also think half the people who use the word don't know what it means either. It can be a valuable tool if understood correctly, but to most it's this process for when you overcook your meat and everything magically reverses to a point where you haven't overcooked it. A bit like time travel. I hate to spoil this idea, but once you've overcooked (I mean cooking at such a high temperature for long enough to lose moisture that you could have saved) your meat, it's overcooked (in the same way that a golf pro will tell you you're over-swinging even when you've just hit a near perfect nine iron six feet from the pin). Some juices do withdraw as meat cools and it can look like it's more even in colour but it's still dryer than it could be. It's better, yes, but not overcooking it is a hell of a lot better. Most of the juice that has dripped into the pan or grill is never coming back into the meat, no matter how hard you try. As meat cools it does act a bit like a sponge but a bad sponge, especially if it's lean.

The real reason we might leave cooked meat to sit for a bit is either because it's not quite fully cooked and it needs to warm itself through from its own thermal energy (I call this 'self-cooking' – it's beneficial for lean meats and small steaks), or it needs to cool down so the melted collagen and fats solidify a bit, meaning when we slice into the meat we don't lose too much of either (this is beneficial in fattier cuts, especially brisket). Resting for low and slow is done whilst cooking; it is the cooking.

If, however, you have a steak that is cooked to your liking, I would suggest slicing and eating it almost straight away. Yes, some juice might run out if you've cooked it a little too hot and fast, but that's not going to make it dry. If it's cooked well, that puddle of meat juice (not blood, blood looks very very different) will be only a fraction of the moisture in the steak, and also makes a lovely sauce to pour back over your sliced, perfectly cooked steak. Much worse is leaving it there to overcook in its own heat.

You might need to nap, your dog certainly needs to nap, but meat doesn't need a nap ever. It's dead – this is its nap.

Internal cooking temperatures

Undercooked meat is something that terrifies customers and consumers. (When I say 'meat', here, I'm referring mainly to red meats. I'll talk about pork later as it's way more controversial.) In fact, just the use of the word 'rare' is largely misunderstood and considered to be undercooked. Most people's opinion of what is undercooked and what isn't is down more to personal preference than to what is best for the meat itself. Fact is, red meat – even when totally raw – is generally perfectly safe for healthy adults to eat as long as the surface of the meat is free from bacteria.

The inside of red meat doesn't have any bacteria, so whether it's stone-cold raw or well-done makes no difference at all to its safety. The only danger point is the surface of the meat itself and as long as we have introduced that to a heat of 73.5°C or above, it is perfectly safe.

For me, undercooked is when the meat is tough and this is dependent on how much connective tissue it has inside. Connective tissue is there because the muscle (which is what meat is) moves around a lot. So the meat next to our joints and legs tends to be tougher than the meat on our belly and back. Muscles that move around a lot also look much darker because they need oxygen, which they get from the blood that flows through them. This is why the meat of wild game birds is darker than that of chickens and geese raised in captivity, which is almost white.

The darker the meat, the more active the animal was, so colour is a decent indicator that it's from an older animal or one that had been out chewing on Mother Nature, roaming free and not stuffed in a cage all its life. In most cases, rich colour means the meat will taste better, although flavour also depends on what the animal had been eating, so it isn't a 100-per-cent-foolproof clue.

With red meat, the toughest cuts either need to be cooked fully or, if you're cheating, sliced paper thin to be edible, whilst the leanest cuts like the fillet, which lies along the back and hardly ever moves, need practically no cooking at all.

In between, there are cuts requiring different levels of cooking to create sufficient tenderness – and this is where it all gets very subjective. The only flavour that cooking adds is on the surface. After that it's all about gaining the right texture.

A question I always ask is why cook fillet any more than blue or rare? It's soft enough in its raw state for us to eat without difficulty. So the benefit of cooking it past rare (which means it isn't cold any more) is non-existent. There are no food safety benefits from cooking fillet to medium, even if it did have bacteria. You extract more moisture through cooking it for longer, so it ends up drier and less flavourful.

Rare to well-done

The international parameters for the meaning of 'rare', 'medium-rare', 'medium' and 'well-done' are vague. In the USA, medium-rare steak is considered to be at 58°C internally, which would be called medium in the UK and medium to well-done in some parts of Europe. Also, opinions are skewed by people's misconception of what medium-rare looks like, which is usually down to poor meat cooking. Some consider an overcooked outer layer with a rare centre to be medium-rare. Some people also consider Creationism to be real though, so I guess we have to take people's considerations with a pinch of salt.

Steak cooking is a very personal thing so my rules don't apply to everyone, but in my world the following (see above right) works well. Colour is a decent indicator of these temperatures, but they can vary according to the age and breed of the animal, cooking time and cut.

A temperature guide

Raw	0–29°C (or untouched)
Blue	30–39°C
Rare	40–47°C
Medium-rare	48–56°C
Medium	57–63°C
Medium-well	64–69°C
Well-done	70°C +

Raw

Blue

Rare

Medium

Medium-well

Well-done

How to cook steak

The cooking method here can be used for any boneless steak, be it beef flat iron, sirloin, rib eye, fillet or rump, or a leg, shoulder or skirt steak from any other large animal (e.g. lamb and pork steaks). The only important factor to consider is the thickness of the steak and how you want it cooked (see Different Steaks to Consider, pages 46–50, for advice).

I've mentioned the weight of the steaks in all the following methods to give you an idea of what to order per person, but weight has much less of an impact on how long it takes to cook a steak than thickness.

With this method, and indeed any method, a 3cm-thick 700g cowboy steak (a large but quite thin cross-section cut from the leg) will cook in roughly the same time as a 350g sirloin that is also 3cm thick because it's the depth (thickness) and NOT the width that affects the cooking time. After the searing stage, when it's tempering in the oven, the time for this indirect cooking process will differ with weight but to a much smaller degree than you might expect.

You should be able to specify thickness with your local butcher or even your supermarket. It's also an easier way to order when you don't really have a handle on how much a steak should weigh. For most people, 250g of meat is a good main-course size for one serving. For all the following steaks we will work with the same set up:

1. **PUT YOUR PAN (PREFERABLY CAST IRON) ON A MEDIUM-HIGH HEAT.**
   With most hobs, turn the dial three-quarters of the way to full heat and leave for at least 10 minutes. If you have a probe, the pan will be roughly 150–180°C when ready. If you don't have a probe, add a little flavourless oil to the pan: it should smoke lightly when the pan is hot enough.

2. **SET YOUR OVEN TO COOK AT 120°C.**
   An oven thermometer is useful. My oven is about 5°C lower in temperature than the setting on my dial, and it wildly fluctuates between 116° and 122°C even with the door closed, as most ovens do. If your oven is too hot or too cold, adjust the temperature accordingly, although in theory the difference will only account for minutes in cooking time so shouldn't skew your results too much.

3. **PLACE A ROASTING/BAKING TRAY IN THE OVEN WHILST IT'S HEATING UP.**
   I never use the pan I'm searing a steak in to cook my meat in the oven. It's too hot and will continue to sear the meat, creating an uneven cook. When I place it in the oven, I want it to be at a lower temperature or the same temperature as the oven.

4. **HAVE SOME SEA SALT AND A NEUTRAL OIL TO HAND.**
   If you feel like upping your game, use some good-quality unsalted butter instead of oil. I use grass-fed butter for all my cooking, which is much better for you than a lot of oils and adds better flavour. You will also need some tongs and a plate for when your steak comes out of the oven.

5. **TAKE YOUR STEAK OUT OF THE FRIDGE AND ADD IT STRAIGHT TO THE PAN.** When you initially sear the steak, the internal temperature is lower, which will give you more time to sear whilst still keeping the meat from overcooking. The longer the sear time, the deeper the colour and therefore the greater the flavour (see page 18 for more info on searing). Press the steak down using your fingers or tongs so that all of the surface comes into contact with the hot pan.

6. **MOVE YOUR STEAK AROUND THE PAN CONSTANTLY AND FLIP IT OVER REGULARLY.** Flip and season the hot side, then repeat the flipping every 1–2 minutes or when you can't hear any sizzling. The sizzle is your guide to tell you the steak is searing properly – when it goes quiet, move it. You will only need to season each side once or twice lightly with salt. (See page 19 for why moving and flipping is good.) If the heat in the pan drops too much so you're not getting the best colour, turn up the temperature but be careful of the colour becoming black. If it does, remove the steak from the pan, turn down the heat and wait for the pan to cool a bit before placing the steak back in. At the end of the pan-cooking, the internal temperature of your steak will be roughly 30°C.

Small steak

Medium steak

Large steak

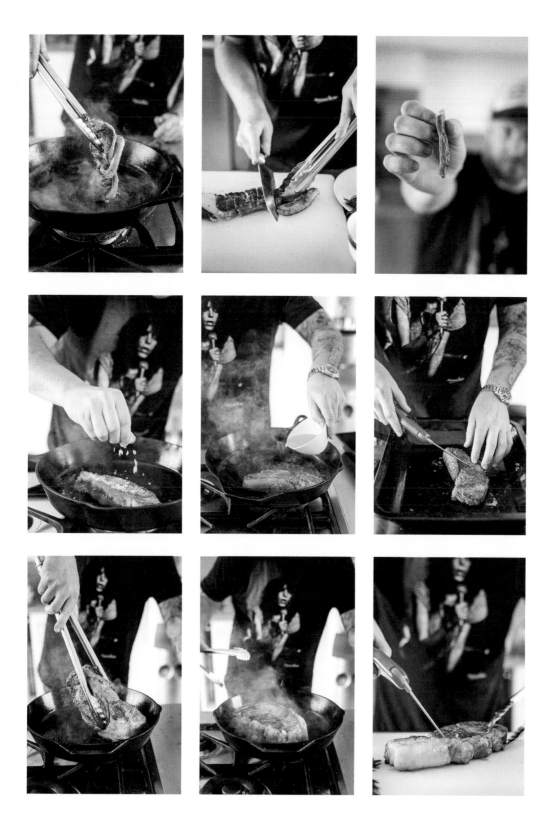

Small steak

90G, LESS THAN 1CM THICK

Small steaks can be really hard to cook evenly, and their lack of depth doesn't give you the time to build up flavour through colour. So in order to buy more time you need this steak to start as cold as possible. Fridge temperatures are simply not cold enough so you have to freeze the steak, unless you want it well-done.

Freeze it as flat as possible so that when you start to cook it in the pan it gets as much contact with the heat source as possible. To do this, place the steak on a lightly oiled flat tray or plastic lid.

Brush the top of the steak with a little oil to prevent too much surface ice from forming, then put it directly into your freezer and leave for at least an hour.

Get your pan to the right temperature (see page 34). A ridged griddle pan is ideal for this as you get good contact despite any moisture from the freezing process, but a flat pan will do fine. You don't need the oven for steaks this thin.

Remove the steak from the freezer and immediately place it in the pan. Set a heavy saucepan or other suitable object on top of the steak to keep it flat (I use my hands but you might not want to get your hands that close to the hot pan).

Leave it like this for about 30 seconds to get a good sear – don't be afraid to push it down a lot as this is all about contact. You won't lose any moisture as the steak is still frozen inside.

Now take a pair of tongs and flip the steak over and then over again, into a different area of the pan each time, for 2–3 minutes for rare. Slice straight away to stop the cooking.

For medium-rare, remove the steak from the pan and let it self-cook for 2 minutes, then slice immediately. For medium, self-cook for 4 minutes before slicing. The slicing will stop the cooking, which is important.

You'll note I didn't season this steak at all during the cooking. You can season during the flipping stage, but for me doing it after slicing provides just as much seasoning without the hassle.

Medium steak

250G, 2-3CM THICK

Heat the pan and turn your oven to cook at 120°C, with a roasting/baking tray inside (see page 34).

Cook the steak straight from the fridge. If the steak has a layer of fat on its side, start by rendering this out in the hot pan to create a layer of fat. To do this, hold the steak on its edge with a pair of tongs and press the fat into the pan to melt it, or prop the steak against the side of the pan (see page 36). If the steak is lean, with no fat layer, put a very small amount of neutral oil in the pan to prevent initial sticking.

Sear the steak for up to 5 minutes or until you have a good brown crust covering the bulk of it. Flip and move it every 30 seconds, or when you don't hear a sizzle, seasoning each side only once (see page 30). Make sure you don't ignore the edges. After 4 minutes, an optional touch is to add a dollop of clarified butter or rendered fat and use it to gain that last hit of colour.

Once the steak has been seared, transfer it to the heated tray in the oven. Put the pan, with all the juices, to one side.

Once in the oven...

- For rare, cook for 1–2 minutes.
- For medium-rare, cook for 3–5 minutes.
- For medium, cook for 8–10 minutes.

Slice the steak immediately and season lightly with extra crushed sea salt plus some pepper, if you like, then drizzle over the juices from the pan.

Large steak

500G, 4-5CM THICK

Before cooking, it's wise to bash out the steak to 3–4cm thickness (see page 28). Whilst this does reduce the cooking time slightly, it's not the same as cooking a 3cm steak as the heat doesn't transfer through the meat fibres in a straight line. Bashing out will reduce the pan-searing time and give you more surface area to sear, thus giving you more flavour.

Heat the pan and turn your oven to cook at 120°C with a roasting/baking tray inside (see page 34).

Cook the steak straight from the fridge. If the steak has a layer of fat on its side, start by rendering this out in the hot pan to create a layer of fat. To do this, hold the steak on its edge with a pair of tongs and press the fat into the pan to melt it, or prop the steak against the side of the pan (see page 36). If the steak is lean, with no layer of fat, put a very small amount of neutral oil in the pan to prevent initial sticking.

Sear the steak for up to 5 minutes or until you have a good brown crust covering the bulk of it. Flip and move it every 30 seconds, or when the sizzle dies, seasoning each side only once (see page 30). Make sure you don't ignore the edges. After 4 minutes, an optional touch is to add a dollop of clarified butter or rendered fat and use it to gain that last hit of colour.

Once the steak has been seared all over, transfer it to the hot tray in the oven. Put the pan, with the juices, to one side.

Once in the oven …

- For rare, cook for 10–12 minutes.
- For medium-rare, cook for 18–20 minutes.
- For medium, cook for 28–30 minutes.

Slice the steak immediately and season lightly with extra crushed sea salt plus some pepper if you like, then drizzle over the juices from the pan.

Very large steak

1 KG, 7-8CM THICK

Almost the size of a roast, this is a monster steak and great for impressing a group of friends. Bash it out to 5–6cm thickness and also try the roughing-up (or scraping) method (page 28).

Heat the pan and turn your oven to cook at 120°C with a roasting/baking tray inside (see page 34).

Cook the steak straight from the fridge. For a steak this size, it's likely to be a sirloin or a rib eye unless it's from a dinosaur. If it's a sirloin, start by rendering out the fat layer in the hot pan (for more about the fat on a sirloin steak, see page 46). To do this, hold the steak on its edge with a pair of tongs and press the fat into the pan to melt it, or prop the steak against the side of the pan. If it's a rib eye, put it straight in the pan (its fat content means you don't need any oil).

Sear the steak for up to 6 minutes or until you have a good brown crust covering the bulk of it. The sheer weight of this steak should mean it gets a good contact with the hot pan, so there's no need to push down too hard. Flip every minute, seasoning each side only once (see page 30). Make sure you don't ignore the edges. After 5 minutes, add a dollop of clarified butter or rendered fat if you like, and use it to gain that last hit of colour.

Once the steak has been seared, transfer it to the hot tray in the oven. Put the pan, with the juices, to one side.

Once in the oven ...

- For rare, cook for 18–20 minutes.
- For medium-rare, cook for 28–30 minutes.
- For medium, cook for 36–38 minutes.

Slice the steak immediately and season lightly with extra crushed sea salt plus some pepper if you like, then drizzle over the juices from the pan.

Different steaks to consider

BEEF STEAKS

As mentioned on page 44, with a **sirloin** steak you need to render out the fat layer on the edge first. Apart from that, the cooking is pretty similar to that for fillet as they're both very lean. I love the fat. It's my favourite part of the steak, so I'm not into rendering it out too much, just getting it to crisp up. But I know I'm in a minority, so if you have a heavy fat layer, try starting with a cooler pan (less than 130°C) and leave the steak on its fat edge for longer. You can then pour out the excess fat and keep it for later. Alternatively, you can just trim back the fat with a knife before cooking.

Most sirloins are thicker per gram than rib eye or other cuts, so large sirloin steaks are the best for bashing out.

I think sirloin should be cooked rare to medium-rare. Any more and the internal fat content won't be enough to stop it drying out. There is very little collagen to cook out so a long cooking time isn't necessary.

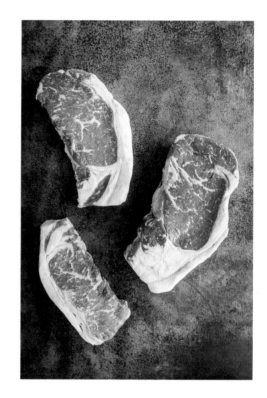

Rib eye is the perfect steak for home cooking. You get a great surface area to build colour, and the fat content is high enough that you won't need any oil in the pan, ever.

The only problem with cooking rib eye is that it is made up of two different muscle groups – the internal round eye or fillet and the outer section called the deckle – but they can be easily separated just by pulling them apart (see photo below right). Make sure that you push down on both parts to get surface contact with the hot pan. If you have a thermometer and find that the fillet and deckle are not cooking evenly, you can always separate them midway through and cook them separately. In reality, though, it's never a big issue unless you're shooting for absolute perfection.

Medium-rare to medium is perfect for this cut. If you're a fan of medium-well or well-done, we're not friends anymore – but this is a decent cut for you to use.

Outside fine dining, a lot of modern chefs tend to shy away from **fillet** steak. It's expensive and its shape is awkward for even cooking: you need to concentrate on the sides just as much as the top and bottom. But I have a soft spot for a great piece of fillet. Unlike a sirloin steak, I don't recommend bashing it out as it will look like a crumpled can of Coke and you won't get contact colour in the creases. Also, fillet is an extremely delicate meat.

A whole fillet is a long cylinder that is thin at one end and very thick at the other. The two ends need different cooking techniques: for steaks from the thin end, you're concentrating on the sides, whereas for the thicker-end steaks, it's the top and bottom because that's where the larger surface area is. However, the basic cooking principles are the same as for all steaks.

I think fillet should be cooked rare or even blue. For a thin-end steak, you could do the pan work described for a small steak for up to 5 minutes, then just leave it at room temperature for a few minutes to self-cook in its own heat. For me this gives a perfect result. Steaks from the middle and thick end weighing 250g might need 1–2 minutes in the oven.

For those who want to cook fillet any further than rare, please note that you don't need to cook this steak at all as it's tender enough raw. Remember that we're only cooking to achieve tenderness and preserve moisture content. That's the goal. There are no extra food safety benefits between a rare steak and a medium steak. (If food safety is your worry, you'll need to cook everything well-done or eat a salad instead.) As long as the outside is seared to a high temperature, that's all the cooking you really need for a tasty fillet.

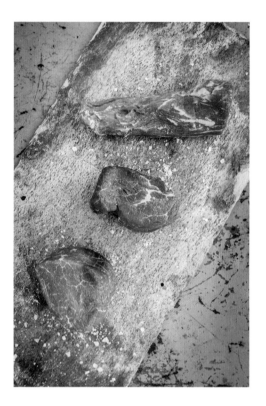

Lamb chop

Pork chop

Sirloin

Bavette

Onglet

Fillet

Fillet

Rump

Mince

Fillet

Rib eye

The **bavette**, which is generally around 2cm thick, is the thick part of the abdominal muscle of the cow near the leg. It has the same texture as the rest of the meat from that area, which is made up of long, thick strands of muscle fibre with interwoven fat and collagen. The muscle itself is a lot tougher than lean cuts such as fillet and sirloin, but it isn't filled with so much heavy collagen that it needs to be fully cooked like the brisket or leg meat.

Some people like to marinate bavette to soften the tissue, but in truth, it's better to cook it medium-rare and just accept that the slight chewiness is actually part of its appeal. When you've cooked it, slice it thinly at right angles to the grain to make it even more tender when eating.

Also known as hanger steak because of the way it hangs off the diaphragm near the top of the front leg, an **onglet** steak is generally 2–3cm thick.

Like the bavette, the strands of muscle fibre are thick, so onglet has a little chew to it, but this is made up for by an intense gaminess that isn't found in any other muscle. It is a great cut of beef that is good value and has lots of uses. Sliced thinly, onglet is great in tacos and stir-fries as well as quick-cook stews.

The only problem when cooking an onglet steak is its odd shape. It's almost round so doesn't have any real sides, which makes it difficult to cook evenly. To get some good browning surfaces, bash it out a little first with a heavy saucepan to give you two flat sides, and ideally cook it medium-rare or medium.

PORK, VEAL OR LAMB CHOPS

I'm not a fan of steaks with bones but I love a **chop**. It does present a few hurdles though because of the bone. The first issue is contact with the hot pan because no matter how well the chop has been cut, once cooking has started the flesh will pull back from the bone, making it harder to get good contact to sear and gain colour. The best way to combat this is to place a heavy object (such as a clean brick, a heavy pan or any clean, heatproof weight) on top of the meaty part of the chop at the start of cooking to push down the flesh to meet the pan.

For me, rare for lamb is like medium-rare for beef in that the moisture content is similar and they look consistent in colour balance. Lamb also has great fat flavour and is the one meat that still tastes good cooked through – meaning that if you take it a little too far, it's not really a big issue.

Veal and pork I treat like beef, but I accept not everybody has my faith in pink pork, so you may want to take it to medium or even medium-well.

BURGERS

The cooking of **burgers** almost warrants its own book. For something so everyday and taken for granted, there are innumerable ways people cook them, whether it's steaming, grilling, smashing on a griddle or pan-frying. Everyone has an opinion and a method, and none of them is totally right or wrong… except mine, which is the best way ever to cook a burger.

To start off you have to get the right mince. Don't just buy some ready-minced rubbish from the supermarket. Mince

is cheap, even the good stuff, so go to a trusted butcher. Ask him for twice coarsely ground (6–8mm plate) mince from a good animal. Well-aged beef is great if that's your bag but it's all down to personal preference. The cut matters less than people make out but you do want it to be at least 15–20 per cent fat. If the butcher asks you what cut, brisket, chuck, shortrib, rib eye cap, plate or blade are all good choices. Avoid fillet and sirloin because they are too lean and too expensive – as you're mincing the meat, the tenderness you'd pay for is pointless. Shin and leg cuts have a little too much tough collagen even after mincing. Absolutely do not use expensive Waygu beef (see page 17) – that would be insanity as what you'd be paying for is internal marbling. When you mince Waygu, the fat is no longer internal and therefore the initial structure is pointless. Buy cheap cuts from well-looked-after cows.

Don't add anything to your mince and don't play about with it too much. When you're ready to cook, get your pan a little hotter than for a steak as there will be a lot of initial fat rendering, which will cool everything down. Set your oven to 120°C and put a roasting/baking tray in the oven to heat up.

Grab a handful (160–200g) of mince and GENTLY shape it into a rough ball with one motion. Then press it with the flat of your hand against a plate to around 1.8cm thickness. It will not be a perfect circle and that's fine. It may even have some cracks and bits looking like they are going to fall off, which is also fine. Season liberally with fine salt on the side facing up and then wash your hands. Pick up the burger with a spatula and place it salted side down in the pan with no oil. Gently press it down a little, then leave it. Once you can see a dark brown crust appearing on the contact side (or the burger has been cooking for 3 minutes), salt the other side, then flip it. Cook for 2 more minutes. The burger will now be rare.

Transfer the burger to the heated tray in the oven and cook for:

- 5 minutes for medium-rare.
- 11 minutes for medium.

This cooking technique is all about crust development and texture variance. The inside should be soft and juicy, the outside should have a hard satisfying crunch. Don't listen to anyone who tells you all the fibres should be in line and all the surfaces perfectly flat. That reduces the surface area and makes a boring lifeless burger. You want it to be literally falling apart and ugly. The uglier the better.

SAUCES, BUTTERS

AND SIDES

FOR STEAKS

These recipes are for garnishes and accompaniments that you can pair with your steak. I've tried to keep them simple yet interesting and to use flavours you might not expect with steaks. Béarnaise and chips is a classic I go back to time and time again, but sometimes I like a change. I hope you enjoy these as much as I do.

Basic Hollandaise

SERVES 4 - 6

This is a basic hot emulsion that goes well with any meat. The butter should be the main flavour, with an acidity coming from the lemon and white wine reduction. I use bay rather than tarragon because I prefer the flavour, but you can use any herb as long as the result is subtle. The secrets to any emulsion are speed and temperature. As butter gets colder it solidifies, which in turn can split the sauce. Alternatively, if it gets too hot the same thing will happen as the eggs will overcook and scramble. Rule of thumb is to keep checking the sauce with your finger: it should feel warm at all times. If it's too hot to touch, take it off the heat; if it's cold, turn the heat up a little.

200ml white wine (cheap stuff from a box is fine)
200ml white wine vinegar
1 teaspoon black peppercorns
1 garlic clove, crushed
1 bay leaf (break the leaf to release more flavour)
4 free-range egg yolks (at room temp)
50ml milk (at room temp)
200g unsalted butter, melted (no need to clarify)
Juice of 1 lemon
Maldon salt and pepper

Start by reducing the white wine and vinegar with the peppercorns, garlic and bay in a pan. There is no rule as to how much you should reduce by but over half should work fine. The purpose is to infuse the reduction, burn off alcohol and intensify flavour so you need less liquid in the mix. I sometimes use just white wine and it works fine. Once reduced, strain the liquid and cool a little.

Take another pan and add a little water, then set a heatproof bowl on the top – the base shouldn't touch the water. Place your egg yolks in the bowl and add a pinch of salt, the milk and a couple of tablespoons of the reduction – less if you want a less acidic result or more if you like it sharper. Remember that you can always add more reduction later on to balance the flavour, so go light at first.

Get mixing straight away off the heat, then put the pan on the heat and slowly turn it up. Whisk furiously, trying to get as much air into the eggs as possible. The milk will help to loosen the mix and stabilise the emulsion. You want to take it as far as you can without it scrambling, although a little cooked egg will be okay, so don't be too afraid. When you can lift up the whisk and draw a number 8 with the mix that falls back into the bowl, you're ready to add the butter.

Hollandaise

Kimchi Hollandaise

Béarnaise

Charcoal Béarnaise

Basic Hollandaise continued

Remove the pan from the heat and lift off the bowl. Lay a towel over the pan and replace the bowl – the towel will hold the bowl in place as you need both hands for the next stage. With one hand, pour the melted butter into the egg mix in a steady stream (you can add the milk solids too), whilst with the other hand, whisk using a back and forth motion as fast as you can. The faster you do this, the better. Stop when you're happy with the consistency of the sauce.

Season the sauce with the lemon juice, salt and a little pepper. If you think the sauce is too thick, add some lukewarm water; if it's too thin, add more melted butter. Keep the sauce in a warm place (like set in another bowl filled with warm water) and serve as soon as possible.

Kimchi Hollandaise

SERVES 4-6

This makes more kimchi paste than you need for this sauce, but it's a great stock item to have in your kitchen. Store it in your fridge and it will last for months. You can use it to make your own kimchi or add it to other dishes (see Fresh Apple Kimchi, page 254).

200ml white wine (cheap stuff from a box is fine)
200ml white wine vinegar
4 free-range egg yolks (at room temp)
50ml milk (at room temp)
200g unsalted butter, melted (no need to clarify)
Juice of 1 lemon
Maldon salt and pepper

FOR THE KIMCHI PASTE
50g gochugaru (Korean chilli powder)
50g salted shrimps
50g drained tinned brown anchovy fillets in oil
50g peeled garlic
50g peeled fresh ginger
50g light soft brown sugar
50ml soy sauce
2 fresh green chillies

Put all the ingredients for the kimchi paste in a blender or food prosessor and blitz until smooth, scraping down the sides of the goblet from time to time.

Make a Basic Hollandaise (see page 54) – you can leave out the garlic, bay and peppercorns from the reduction as their flavours won't come through in this sauce. Add 2 tablespoons of the kimchi paste to the finished sauce, which will turn it a nice dark orange, almost red colour. Serve as soon as possible.

Basic Béarnaise

SERVES 4 - 6

This is great with any meat but I reserve it for beef – for me the ultimate meal is béarnaise with steak and chips. There is almost nothing better. The secret to this is getting in as much tarragon flavour as possible.

200ml white wine (cheap stuff from a box is fine)
200ml white wine vinegar
1 teaspoon black peppercorns
1 garlic clove, crushed
1 bay leaf (break the leaf to release more flavour)
1 bunch tarragon
4 free-range egg yolks (at room temp)
50ml milk (at room temp)
200g unsalted butter, melted (no need to clarify)
Juice of 1 lemon
Maldon salt and pepper

Reduce the wine and vinegar with the peppercorns, garlic and bay in the same way as for the Basic Hollandaise (see page 54), but add in the tarragon stalks (reserve the leaves for later). To get more flavour out of the stalks, break them up a little by hand and scrunch them first. Whole herbs impart good flavour but, as with the bay leaf and garlic, crushing them up a bit intensifies it.

Follow all the same steps as for the Basic Hollandaise. Right at the end, chop up the tarragon leaves roughly and mix them through the finished sauce. Serve as soon as possible.

Charcoal Béarnaise

SERVES 4 - 6

This is a great sauce to get that charcoal-grilled flavour into a steak that has been nowhere near a barbecue.

200ml white wine (cheap stuff from a box is fine)
200ml white wine vinegar
1 teaspoon black peppercorns
1 garlic clove, crushed
1 bay leaf (break the leaf to release more flavour)
1 tablespoon chopped tarragon
4 free-range egg yolks (at room temp)
50ml milk (at room temp)
150g unsalted butter, melted (no need to clarify)
Juice of 1 lemon
Maldon salt and pepper

FOR THE CHARCOAL BUTTER
2 pieces of lumpwood charcoal
150g unsalted butter

To make the charcoal butter, burn the charcoal either on a BBQ or on your gas stove until glowing hot. Melt the butter in a pan, then remove from the heat. Immerse the hot coals in the butter and cover the pan immediately. The charcoal flavour needs to infuse the butter, so leave the pan covered until it stops smoking and has cooled a little. (Do all this away from a smoke alarm – preferably outside!) Strain the butter.

Make a Basic Béarnaise (see opposite). Whisk in about 50g of the charcoal butter along with the normal melted butter. Add as much charcoal butter as you like – it has an intense flavour, so taste as you go. Serve as soon as possible.

Bone-marrow Béarnaise

SERVES 4 - 6

Here is a punchy, beefy sauce that will complement steak brilliantly.

100g bone marrow (out of
    the bone)
100g unsalted butter
200ml white wine (cheap
    stuff from a box is fine)
200ml white wine vinegar
1 teaspoon black
    peppercorns
1 garlic clove, crushed
1 bay leaf (break the leaf to
    release more flavour)
1 bunch tarragon
4 free-range egg yolks
    (at room temp)
50ml milk (at room temp)
Juice of 1 lemon
Maldon salt and pepper

Chop up the bone marrow and melt it down with the butter in a pan.

Make a Basic Béarnaise (see page 58), whisking in the bone marrow-butter mixture. Serve as soon as possible.

A1 Hollandaise

SERVES 4 - 6

This sauce is not only great with steaks but is heaven in a bacon sandwich. A1 is an American steak sauce that is available to buy online or in some supermarkets in the UK. You can use HP Sauce instead if you are struggling to find A1.

200ml white wine (cheap stuff from a box is fine)
1 teaspoon black peppercorns
1 garlic clove, crushed
1 bay leaf (break the leaf to release more flavour)
100ml A1 Steak Sauce (or HP Sauce plus a splash of Tabasco sauce)
4 free-range egg yolks (at room temp)
50ml milk (at room temp)
200g unsalted butter, melted (no need to clarify)
Juice of 1 lemon
Maldon salt and pepper

Follow the procedure for making a Basic Hollandaise (see page 54) but make the reduction with wine alone rather than wine and vinegar, and mix the A1 sauce with the strained reduction. Serve as soon as possible.

Chimichurri

SERVES 4 - 6

There are many variations of this Argentinian steak sauce. I prefer it kept a little chunky and loose, but you can also stick it all in a blender or food processor and make a smoother sauce.

2 red onions, finely diced
2 garlic cloves, finely diced
½ tablespoon chopped
    tarragon
½ tablespoon dried oregano
½ tablespoon chopped mint
2 tablespoons chopped
    parsley
100ml vegetable oil
Juice of 2 limes
Juice of ½ lemon
2 teaspoons light soft
    brown sugar
1 tablespoon sherry vinegar
½ teaspoon paprika
Maldon salt

Simply mix together all the ingredients. Don't be too shy to go extra-heavy on the herbs and lime. You can also play around with different herbs.

This sauce can be kept for a few weeks in the fridge but will lose its vibrancy and freshness, so should ideally be consumed on the day it is made.

Mushroom and bone-marrow butter

Chimichurri

Mushroom and bone-marrow butter

SERVES ABOUT 10

Umami-rich and meaty, this is my ultimate flavoured butter for steak. You can make a butter like this with lots of different ingredients, and it's easy, but I think this is the only one you'll ever need. Serve a dollop on top of a hot steak or spread on toast for a great steak sandwich.

100g bone marrow (out of the bone)
200g portobello mushrooms (or any good mushrooms, even a mix), chopped into rough 1cm dice
50ml soy sauce
50ml sherry vinegar
200g unsalted butter (softened to room temp)
2 garlic cloves, grated or finely chopped
Grated zest of ½ lemon
1 tablespoon chopped parsley
Maldon salt and pepper

In a pan, melt the bone marrow until it starts to sizzle. Add the mushrooms with a pinch of salt and cook them down until the liquid from them has evaporated, stirring as soon as they start to stick but not before. You want to end up with a deep, deep colour and lots of brown sticky stuff on the bottom of the pan.

Once you have enough colour, deglaze with the soy sauce and reduce until it's nearly evaporated, then repeat with the vinegar. Remove from the heat and leave to cool completely before roughly pulsing in a blender or food processor.

Add the marrow-mushroom mix to the soft butter along with the rest of the ingredients and mix together well. Season with salt and pepper. Place in a container and chill in the fridge until set. This can be kept for a number of weeks in the fridge or even frozen.

Foie gras sauce

SERVES 4 - 6

This is a rich and indulgent sauce that has to be made just before serving – if you try to cool and reheat it, it will split more times than not. But it's so worth the last-minute prep. The sauce can also be made with chicken or duck livers, using the same quantities.

300g fresh foie gras lobe,
    cut into thick slices
50ml brandy
300ml double cream
2 bay leaves
½ lemon
Maldon salt and cayenne
    pepper

Get a pan super hot before you start to add your foie gras. Do this bit by bit so you don't overcrowd the pan. You want to get a really good colour, not only on the foie gras but also a build up of brown sticky goodness on the bottom of the pan. If it starts to get too dark, take the pan off the heat and add a splash of water to deglaze. Once you have enough colour, remove the foie gras and deglaze the pan with the brandy, stirring well to mix in all the sticky sediment.

Reduce the brandy down until it is almost gone, then add back the foie gras along with the cream and bay leaves. Reduce the cream, stirring all the time, until it thickens and the flavour of the sauce has intensified.

Add salt and cayenne to taste and finish with a squeeze of lemon. Serve immediately or as soon as possible.

Red onion pickle

MAKES A LARGE BATCH

This is a basic pickling recipe that can be used for almost any veg. With red onion it's quick and easy, and it looks vibrant. The pickle is also great in sandwiches or salads or as an accompaniment to cured meat or fish. It can be kept in the fridge for months.

3 red onions, finely sliced
200ml white wine vinegar
200ml cold water
480g caster sugar
1 teaspoon fennel seeds
1 bay leaf
½ teaspoon coriander seeds

Put the onions in a bowl. Heat the rest of the ingredients together in a pan, stirring to dissolve the sugar, until just about to simmer.

Remove from the heat and leave to infuse for 15 minutes, then strain on to the onions. Leave to pickle for at least 2–3 hours. Before serving, strain off the pickling juice (you can keep this to pickle something else).

Oyster tartare

SERVES 2-4

Oysters and steak are a marriage made in heaven. This recipe just takes a traditional oyster garnish and makes it into a sauce.

6 fresh oysters, shucked
(keep the juices from
the shells)
2 teaspoons finely diced
Red Onion Pickle (see
page 65)
2 teaspoons finely
chopped dill
Juice of ½ lemon
Few drops of Tabasco sauce

Chop up the oysters roughly and place in a bowl. Mix in the red onion pickle and dill. Add lemon juice and Tabasco to your taste and season with a little of the salty oyster juices. Serve as soon as possible.

Green peppercorn sauce

SERVES 2 - 4

This is a sauce to be made after frying your steak, taking advantage of all the sticky browned bits of protein stuck to the bottom of the pan.

1 shallot, finely chopped
250ml port
500ml beef or chicken stock
250ml double cream
100g drained brined green
    peppercorns, roughly
    chopped
50g drained capers,
    chopped
Juice of ½ lemon
Maldon salt

Once your steak is in the oven, drain off any excess oil or fat from the pan, then add the shallot with a small pinch of salt. Stir and soften for a few minutes. Add the port and reduce to a thick glaze. Next add the stock and again boil until syrupy. Pour in the cream and boil until you have a good sauce consistency. Add the peppercorns and capers, and season with a squeeze or two of lemon juice plus salt if necessary. Serve as soon as possible.

Aged beef mayo

SERVES 4-6

This is the king of all mayonnaises, with the taste of aged beef to boost the flavour of your steaks. Serve it alongside or use as a coleslaw dressing. The mayo isn't actually made with aged beef or beef fat, but with an oil that has been infused with aged beef trimmings. A good butcher will have lots of these lying around. You want the super funky black stuff he throws away after the dry-ageing process. Unless he's mean he should give it to you for free. Bits of fat and meat attached are fine. Just make sure it's not too fat-heavy.

4 free-range egg yolks
2 teaspoons Dijon mustard
1 tablespoon white wine
    vinegar
Juice of ½ lemon
Maldon salt and pepper

FOR THE BEEF OIL
250g aged beef trimmings
500ml vegetable oil

To make the beef oil, get a pan nice and hot, then colour your trimmings for a few minutes. Pour in the oil and cook on a medium heat until you start to smell the aroma from the oil. Remove from the heat, cover and leave to cool. The longer you leave the oil cooling, the better the flavour. I would recommend at least 24 hours in the fridge, but you can use the oil after a few hours if you're in a rush. Pass through a fine sieve before using.

You can make the mayonnaise in a blender or using a whisk. Blitz or whisk up your yolks with the mustard and a little salt, then begin adding your beef oil in a slow steady stream, blitzing/whisking until the mix starts to thicken. If it gets too thick, add a little room-temperature water.

Once you have a good consistency, add the vinegar and lemon juice to taste. Season with salt until the beef flavour gets good and strong, and don't be shy to go heavy on the pepper. This can be kept for up to 3 days in the fridge.

Lamb sauce

SERVES 10

Lamb has powerful flavours so, unlike some meats, it can take a belting sauce like this one and still hold its own. This recipe makes a large batch because anything smaller would be difficult in a blender. It's best used on the day it's made.

150g peeled garlic
150g good-quality tinned
    brown anchovy fillets
    in oil
75g parsley (stalks and all)
Juice of 3 small lemons
    (or 2 large)
1 fresh red chilli, chopped
300ml vegetable oil
Maldon salt

Blanch the peeled garlic cloves three times: put them in a pan of cold water, bring to the boil and drain, then repeat. After the third blanching, the garlic should be soft.

Tip the drained garlic into a blender or food processor and add the rest of the ingredients (the anchovy oil can go in too). Blitz to make a smooth, thick sauce. Chill before use. If the sauce splits a little, you can re-blend.

Smacked cucumber

SERVES 2-4

This is a slight twist on a classic Sichuan garnish, particularly good with pork and beef. The cucumber brings a freshness that holds up to the chilli heat. To give this a more traditional flavour, you can replace the sriracha and garlic with 1 tablespoon Chinese chilli-garlic paste, which is available in most supermarkets. Also try dried Sichuan chillies, if you can source them.

1 cucumber
1 tablespoon Maldon sea
    salt
½ tablespoon finely
    chopped garlic
½ tablespoon finely
    chopped fresh ginger
1 tablespoon soy sauce
½ tablespoon sesame oil
½ tablespoon rice wine
    vinegar
½ tablespoon sriracha
    (hot chilli sauce)
2 teaspoons chilli flakes

Bash the cucumber with a heavy object, such as a rolling pin or the back of a heavy pan, to break the cucumber. Split it into four lengthways, then chop into large bite-sized chunks. Mix the cucumber with the salt in a bowl and leave for 10–20 minutes.

Drain the cucumber, then mix with all the other ingredients. You can serve this straight away or it can be kept in the fridge for up to a week.

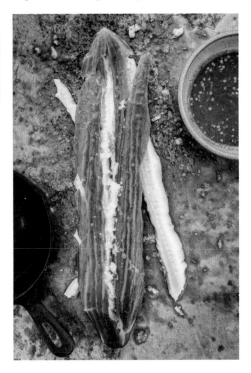

Salted tomatoes with sesame, red onion and bone marrow

SERVES 2 - 4

The contrast between the freshness of tomatoes and the richness of bone marrow works really well as a side to any steak or fish dish. You could leave out the marrow and just use a little olive oil, but it's way more fun and interesting with it. The secret here is to use the best in-season tomatoes and a good sea salt. The better the tomatoes, the less salt you need.

2–3 cross-cut veal or
    young beef bones
4 large beef tomatoes (or
    equivalent)
1 red onion, diced
2 teaspoons toasted sesame
    seeds
Maldon sea salt

Heat your oven to 190°C. Place the bones in a roasting tin and roast for about 20 minutes or until the marrow is soft in the middle but not collapsed. Leave to cool a little, then remove the marrow from the bones and roughly chop with a knife.

Cut your tomatoes into rough 1cm dice and season them fairly liberally with sea salt. Gently mix the marrow and onion through the tomatoes, then sprinkle with the sesame seeds. Serve as soon as possible.

Kimchi fried onions

SERVES 2-4

Caramelised onions are great by themselves or with a splash of vinegar added. This recipe gives them an extra tickle of spice and heat, which elevates them to another level. Serve as a garnish to any meat or fish dish or mix with some fried potatoes.

Vegetable oil, for frying
4 onions, thinly sliced
½ tablespoon Kimchi Paste
  (see page 57)
2 teaspoons black sesame
  seeds
1 spring onion, thinly sliced
Maldon salt

Get a saucepan smoking hot, then add a little oil before throwing in the onions with a pinch of salt. Leave them until they start to stick, then stir well, scraping up the caramelisation on the bottom of the pan as you go. Keep cooking the onions, watching all the time and stirring when necessary, until they are a deep brown. Take them as far as you think you can.

Remove from the heat and stir in the kimchi paste. Serve warm sprinkled with the sesame seeds and spring onion.

'Nduja and crushed roast potato hash

SERVES 4

'Nduja is a spicy Italian sausage similar in flavour to chorizo but with a little more kick. Its higher fat content makes it spreadable and meltable. Hashes can be made with boiled and mashed potatoes, but here I've used crushed leftover roast potatoes. They give a nice crispy texture, plus the inside soaks up the flavour from the 'nduja.

10 leftover cold roast
    potatoes (see page 128)
Oil for deep-frying, plus
    a little extra
1 onion, thinly sliced
50g unsalted butter, plus
    a little extra
100g 'nduja (Italian
    sausage)
Juice of 1 lemon
4 duck eggs
2 tablespoons chopped
    parsley
Maldon salt

Break up the potatoes into smaller pieces – not too small and not too even. You want random chunks. Heat some oil in a deep-fat fryer or deep pan to 180°C. Deep-fry the potatoes until they are crispy. Drain.

Cook the onion in a hot frying pan with a little oil until soft and a good dark colour. Add the potatoes and then the butter. Toss the potatoes in the butter as it melts and foams. Add the 'nduja and stir it in until it melts and coats the potatoes. Season with salt to taste and add a squeeze of lemon. Transfer to individual serving bowls or plates.

Using the same pan, quickly fry the eggs in a little extra oil or butter, keeping the yolks nice and runny. Place an egg on top of each serving of hash and sprinkle with parsley. Serve immediately.

Beef-fat fries

SERVES 4 - 6

I warn you: once you try these, no other chip will ever come close. For the beef fat you'll need to go to your butcher. I'm guessing he will be glad to get rid of it. The more dry-aged the fat is, the better the chip. You can make these with straight oil and no beef fat, and they'll still be mind-blowing.

1kg peeled Maris Piper
potatoes (or any good
dry-matter spud)
2 litres cold water
1 tablespoon Maldon sea
salt
200ml white wine vinegar
2 litres vegetable oil
2kg aged beef fat
Maldon sea salt

Slice your potatoes into small 8mm batons – you want nice, thin chips. Pour the water into a pan and add the 1 tablespoon salt to make the water sea-salty. Stir in the vinegar, then throw in your potatoes.

Bring to the boil and cook until the chips are soft and giving but not breaking apart. Drain in a colander and cool under running cold water, then pat dry with a tea towel. Spread out on a tray and freeze uncovered.

Heat the oil in a deep-fat fryer or deep pan to 190°C. Deep-fry the chips from frozen for about 2 minutes. They shouldn't colour but should develop a bubbly skin. Lift out of the oil and drain on kitchen paper, then pat dry and freeze once more. Once frozen, you can leave the chips until you need them. Keep the oil.

Heat the beef fat with the oil until the fat has melted. Strain to remove any solids, then pour into the deep-fat fryer. Bring up to 190°C.

Deep-fry the frozen chips until they gain a good colour and the outside becomes crisp. As you lift them out and drain, salt straight away. Serve with some Aged Beef Mayo (see page 68) for an extra beefy hit.

Potato bokkeum

SERVES 2-4

This Korean side dish is quick to prepare and won't overpower the flavour of the meat. I sometimes like to add some chopped red chilli and chopped fresh coriander.

500g peeled Maris Piper potatoes (or any good dry-matter spud)

2 carrots, peeled

Vegetable oil, for frying

2 garlic cloves, finely chopped

1 tablespoon light soft brown sugar

75ml cold water

2 tablespoons soy sauce

1 tablespoon toasted sesame oil

1 teaspoon white sesame seeds

1 spring onion, thinly sliced

Slice the potatoes and carrots into julienne. Put the potatoes in a colander and run cold water over them to wash away the starch. Drain well on a tea towel.

Get a pan medium hot with a little oil and start cooking the potatoes and carrots. Once soft, add the garlic and cook for about a minute.

Add the sugar, water and soy sauce, and cook down until the liquid has evaporated. Remove from the heat and mix in the sesame oil. Sprinkle with the sesame seeds and spring onion, then serve.

Tempura onion bhajis

SERVES 4 - 6

Indian recipes for bhajis would use gram flour and you can too, but I much prefer tempura flour. I've given quantities to make your own if you cannot find it in a shop. You could also make the bhajis with other sliced vegetables, such as potato, fennel or carrot.

Oil, for deep-frying
100g tempura flour (store-bought is fine or make your own – see note below)
200ml ice-cold sparkling water
1 free-range egg
3 onions, thinly sliced
2 tablespoons chopped coriander
Grated zest of 1 lemon
1 fresh red chilli, thinly sliced
Maldon salt

Heat some oil in a deep-fat fryer or deep pan to 180°C.

Put the flour in a bowl and slowly mix in the sparkling water. Crack in your egg and mix. Don't make the batter too smooth – it's better kept a bit lumpy. You want a nice thick batter that will stick to the onions. Add the onions and stir into the batter.

You can cook one bhaji at a time, or several (without crowding the pan). For each one, use tongs or a large spoon to grab a bundle of battered onions. Don't try to be neat – we want lots of texture here, so messy and rough is the way to go. Plunge the bundle of onions into your fryer and hold in the hot oil, with your tongs/spoon, for a few seconds. Take a few drips of batter and pour into the fryer to get some extra texture.

When the bhaji is golden brown, remove it and salt immediately, then throw on some coriander, lemon zest and chilli. Drain for a short while on kitchen paper and serve hot. Repeat to make all your bhajis.

NOTE: To make 100g tempura flour, mix together 75g plain flour, 20g rice flour, 2 tablespoons cornflour, 1 teaspoon baking powder and 1 teaspoon fine salt.

ROASTS

In the UK, a roast dinner is at the heart of most family Sundays or special occasions – I remember our roast dinners at home almost as well as our takeaway curries. Today, just about every pub in Britain cooks a roast dinner on Sunday, so for many chefs, Sundays are all about never-ending tray-loads of roast potatoes and a gravy that's been bubbling away for most of the week. If it hits the right note, a roast can be a thing of beauty, but I'd say that seven times out of ten it's a little on the disappointing side. I think the main problem people have with roasting joints (2–6kg pieces of meat) is the fact that you don't have x-ray vision so you can't see inside the cut. Also, most people don't have a good understanding of how far they should cook a large joint. We regard it as a complex puzzle to solve and approach it with negativity.

How to roast meat

Most cookbooks will advise cooking temperatures of 180°C+ for your Sunday roast. The logic is that such high temperatures will give the roast great colour. At these temperatures, a 2kg joint is going to take about 35 minutes to get to medium-rare, whilst a large bird needs about an hour to get to an ideal core temperature. Advice is then to leave the joint or bird to rest for 15–45 minutes, depending on who you listen to, the theory being that the meat juices need to be redistributed (see more about resting, page 30). Personally, as with steaks, I read that as: you've overcooked the roast. So instead of a cooking method set up to overcook your meat, how about one that cooks it properly in the first place?

This traditional way of roasting is a bit like hitting someone over the head with a stick until they do what you want, then waiting for the bruises to heal. Meat hates being overcooked. The juices need redistributing because at high temperature you lose moisture. If you don't cook at high temperature, or for as long as is usually advised, you won't lose any moisture, so you don't need to redistribute anything.

At the far end of the scale, you could say that the ultimate way to roast a large joint is to colour it, then turn the oven right down to the temperature that you need it to cook to. For example, if you have a large chicken that you want to cook to a breast core temperature of 68°C (as an example temperature only), you would colour it, then turn the oven down to 68°C. The bird won't cook past this temperature but then again it will take a long, long time

to get there. You could cook the chicken overnight but, unless you want to use it first thing in the morning, you'd then have to chill it and reheat it – by which time you could have cooked it from scratch. It's also not necessary either as meat loses moisture more rapidly at about 70°C+ and the longer we cook things at these very low temperatures the more dangers can arise.

When you use a 120°C oven, however, most of the meat will be cooking at below that temperature anyway because of how the heat moves through the tissue, cooling as it gets to the centre, and because of the heat's energy distribution in the oven (see page 20). So we can cook at a medium heat without losing moisture.

To deconstruct the cooking of any large roasting joint: it is exactly the same theory as we have applied to cooking a steak. It's just that it's quite a bit bigger.

We still have to do the three steps:

1. Get colour on to it by searing.
2. Temper it to the right temperature inside.
3. Season it.

That's basically all there is to it. The only difference between a steak and a roasting joint is scale, which means the three steps take a little longer.

To brine or not to brine?

The idea behind brining meat is primarily to add moisture. In basic terms, it uses the salt in the water to break down some of the proteins in the meat, which in turn allows it to absorb water. It does work. Brined meat is significantly more juicy and moist than un-brined meat. So it's an easy question then? Of course we should brine…or should we?

Let's look at that again. We add significant amounts of salted water to make a piece of meat more juicy? *Water? Salt water?!*

When you get a juicy piece of meat, the juice or moisture in that meat isn't plain water. It is internal fats, connective tissue and a few other proteins, which carry flavour. Water is water. So yes, brining adds moisture but it also washes away some of the real flavour to an extent. If the meat has no real flavour for sure, brine away.

If we don't overcook our joint then we don't lose very much moisture at all, so we don't need to brine. So I say: don't bother brining, just don't overcook the meat in the first place. If you want to season in advance, dry cure it with salt instead. If it's big, like a turkey, do this at least 24 hours in advance. You'll get the same effect as with a brined piece of meat and it doesn't pump the meat full of flavour-diluting water. But pre-salting isn't really essential either. You can simply not overcook the meat and season the cuts as you pull them off or carve.

Marinades

I tend not to use marinades at all when I cook. That's not to say they don't have their uses. They do tenderise meats and they do add another level of flavour, but in the context of cooking meat perfectly they get in the way.

Marinades prevent perfect searing of steaks and joints as the meat's surface reaction to heat is affected: if the marinade was sugar-heavy, the surface reaction can be one of intense burning; with a yoghurt-based marinade, the flavour will be more to do with the heat's reaction with the marinade than with the meat itself. Oil-based marinades do nothing for the meat and anyway the oil gets burnt off in the first few seconds of cooking.

As a fan of Indian, Middle Eastern and oriental cooking, I enjoy what marinades do but I prefer to add my flavours post-cooking. Also, from a purist's perspective, I want my meat to taste of meat, especially if it's good meat. I also prefer to tenderise my meat through precision cooking rather than applying an acid-based marinade.

In my years of cooking, I've never needed to marinate any meat to make it tender. I'm not saying it's wrong but I am saying try it both ways first.

Crispy skin

It's easy enough to get crispy skin on any piece of meat. All it takes is the right temperature and time. What's hard, though, is getting a crispy skin and not overcooking the meat. A pork belly roasted to perfection is one thing, but add crispy crackling and you've created something of rare beauty. Most of the time you'll get crackling that's somewhere between chewy and hard. It sticks in your teeth or nearly breaks them.

The skin on a joint looks like it is mostly made of fat, especially if we're talking pork skin, but we know this isn't true because it has a strength to it that fat doesn't have. It's tough and it doesn't render down completely. So it must have some connective proteins in there holding it together, much like meat itself. It also has a water content – we know this because when we salt it, moisture comes out.

Getting a dry skin that looks crispy through straightforward cooking isn't hard in theory. But uneven cooking happens because pieces of skin may be in different shapes and sizes, so the heat applied is rarely consistent. We are also trying to do three things all at once: breaking down the connective proteins within the skin; forcing out the water; and firming it all up by expanding the air within the skin and steaming it from the inside. There is just too much going on at once.

So, to get a crispy skin on your roast, this is what you need to do:

1. The connective proteins are very much like the connective tissues in tough pieces of meat. In order to break them down, you need to lower the temperature and extend the time as you cook the joint or whole bird. The meat will remain moist as it cooks during this time.
2. Then you chill the meat.
3. Finally, you apply an intense heat for a short period of time so that the air and steam inside the skin expands. This will cause the skin to puff up like a balloon, creating dry hard walls now filled with air. It also creates a larger surface area that is uneven, which will give more flavour when it is browned.

We can add a further step and dehydrate the skin by placing it in a low oven (below 100°C) after the initial slow-cook, for a long period of time. What you're left with then is a dry and hard piece of skin. It looks like nothing will be able to expand it. But simply apply very fast and extremely high heat to this skin and it will puff up even more (you can see this process most clearly with pork skin but it happens with all skin, see opposite).

If you do remove the skin from the joint, there is a further and final process, which is used for those super-puffy Mexican chicharrones. Scrape off all the fat before drying out the skin and then cook it at a super high heat in oil. This makes crispy skin a doddle but it does go soft after a while because of its lack of fat.

Low-and-slow cooked and chilled pork skin (right), then dehydrated (middle), and then scraped (left).

The outcome of each method, after the intense heat (step 3) is applied.

Pink pork

The attitude to pork is changing – even the American USDA guidelines were recently revised in light of startling evidence that pork is safer than previously thought. The fact is that the reason most of us overcook pork is based on the fear of Trichinosis, which is perhaps one of the rarest diseases on Earth and virtually unheard of in the UK. In the US, only eight cases were reported after the population consumed over 32 billion kilograms of pork. Draw from that what you will. Hepatitis E is also a concern but only really serious for susceptible people like pregnant women and those with an immune deficiency disease.

It's not for me to say 'eat rare or medium-rare pork' (I am not advising you to do either), but if the pork is of excellent quality and you wish to enjoy it in its best state, then a reverse lottery gamble might be worth the risk. It's really up to you. But I can say without a shadow of a doubt that medium-rare pork is a hundred times more delicious than well-done pork. That's a scientific fact.

Food safety controls are there for a very good reason. On a whole they do a very good job and we are better off having them around. But I think you'll do best by understanding the reasoning behind food safety rules and regulations rather than simply blindly following the advice.

If the Food Standards Agency (FSA) were to monitor our general safety day to day in the same way, we would never do anything, ever. If the FSA were to consider the likelihood of someone being hit by a car, for example, there would be an outright ban on cars or speed limits would be reduced to walking speed; pedestrians would wear crash helmets and full protective gear whilst crossing the road; cycling anywhere would be illegal; and there would be warning signs everywhere. And what about the chance of being hit by a meteorite?

Whether we enjoy skiing down a hill, driving a car, cycling, sunbathing, exercising or having sex, there is always a risk-to-reward ratio in almost everything we choose to do. Eating food is really no different. If you're the sort of person who eats for nutrition only then, no, it's probably not worth the risk. But then again if you are, I doubt you'd be reading this book.

General food safety tips

1. Buy well-reared meat from suppliers you trust. That could be your local butcher or farm shop or your supermarket. Supermarket meat comes under major scrutiny and has improved a lot over the years.
2. The best defence against surface bacteria is heat. Cook meat at more than 73.5°C on the surface for a period of time and eat soon after.
3. Don't leave meat out of the fridge for long periods of time. Leaving any food out at room temperature will encourage bacteria to grow at a faster rate than if it was chilled. If you have to leave meat out, though, don't worry too much – just make sure you give it enough heat on the surface before you eat it.
4. Wash your hands and your work surfaces thoroughly. Most of our food-related illness doesn't come from cooking, it comes from cross-contamination from ourselves, our kitchen equipment or our worktops.

Wash everything with hot water and detergent and use a good sanitiser afterwards.

5. Heat-resistant toxins such as botulism are usually found in tinned foods but they can be a big danger in meat too. Thankfully they are very rare. The bacteria is killed by heat but the spores can survive. The biggest danger with spores is letting them multiply, which only happens if the meat is left too long in a reduced-oxygen environment, with lots of moisture and in danger-zone temperatures. Reducing the moisture/ ph levels and temperature control are the key factors in controlling the growth. Whilst it is something to be aware of, it shouldn't be keeping you from cooking or making you lose any sleep. Any spore can be easily controlled by just not leaving meat out of the fridge for a long period of time.

6. Take a few risks. It sounds odd but the more we expose ourselves to bacteria, the better we are at dealing with it. I'm not saying be dirty, but living in a sanitised bubble won't help you long term either.

Roast methods

The ideas in this section are not necessarily ones that are at first glance convenient, and in some cases they are very far from convenient, but essentially these are methods aimed at achieving perfection with a larger window for success and without fancy equipment and/or techniques.

Poultry

First of all we'll look at poultry roasting, which is very different from other meat roasting. The goal of cooking a good bird is two-fold. First, we need a crisp, well-seasoned, browned skin and second, we want a juicy interior, which basically means we don't overcook the bird.

In order to cook the skin well you need a high heat, but first you need to cook the skin at a lower temperature for a while to break down the skin's internal structure and thus enable the high heat to cook it evenly throughout. You also need the skin to be dry because any moisture will only cook like water and we all know water can never reach a temperature past 100°C (boiling point).

Even if you have a 250°C oven, the temperature of a wet skin is well below that. In order to get the Maillard reaction (see pages 12 and 13) you have to hit at least 125°C for a medium-fast cook (140°C is the ideal but, as we've said before with the whole animal, you can still obtain colour below that, it just takes longer). High-heat cooking will do this itself but if you place a bird in the oven

and it spends 30 minutes drying out the moisture in the skin, this only leaves a small amount of time where the high heat is actually doing its job. It's not a terrible method but it is inefficient, and the length of time required usually ends up drying out the bird.

So in all the following methods for roasting poultry, we have a slow-cooking phase to cook the skin itself, followed by a drying phase, then a high-heat phase to gain the colour and crispness. If you do all of these in succession, the time spent in the oven will inevitably overcook the bird. So instead you need to cool the bird down in between at least some of these steps.

The biggest advantage of this heating-and-cooling process is that the bird almost brines itself with its own juices: as the juices get pushed out gently from the core and then cooled, the salt in the skin moves its own juices internally in the same way that brining adds water. Except that this way it's not water, it's tasty meat juice.

This method might seem contradictory to my stance on resting but the difference here is that we haven't cooked at such a high heat to lose too much moisture and the meat hasn't dried; it's just that this is going to make it even better. The final cook is hot but not long enough or hot enough in the core to push out the moisture, meaning you will get a perfect juicy bird every time. You don't have to cook to any specific internal temperature in the final cook as the core temperature has been reached in the slow cook. The bird just has to be heated to taste and not much more, so 50°C core temperature is enough.

Slutty chicken

PERFECT ROAST CHICKEN 2 KG BIRD, SERVES 3 - 4

For most people, the main problems with roasting chicken is undercooked parts of the inside leg, overcooked breasts or the underside of the breast next to the carcass. This is why I recommend ignoring the advice to truss a chicken and instead just let the legs spread themselves open – this way the heat can get in between rather than having to penetrate from the outside of the leg through the thick muscle. Trussing basically creates a huge unnecessary hurdle and larger muscle mass for heat transfer, in a muscle that can take more heat than the breast. It makes little sense.

Un-trussing the legs will mean they cook first because they become the smallest mass instead of part of the whole bird. This is exactly what you want to happen as you can take the leg meat up to 90°C without it drying out, whereas the breast will dry out once you start going above 73.9°C (which is why the advised temperature guidelines for chicken are not ideal).

Also, don't stuff the cavity with anything, open it as much as you can. You want free-flowing heat to penetrate from the inside out during cooking so the breast will cook more quickly. Heat coming from two opposite directions means it has less distance to travel, as the heat only has to reach the core, not the other side. So the breast cooks faster and we minimise the chances of overcooking. Some people are amazed at the time it takes to cook at this low temperature. These are the two problem areas in undercooked chicken: the inside of the breast and the area between the thigh and the body. Solved just by spreading the legs and widening the hole as much as you can. Hence, a 'slutty' chicken…I'm so, so sorry.

STEP 1: COOK AND DRY

Set your oven to 110°C. Leave your bird in the fridge until it's needed. Once the oven is at temperature, take out the bird (un-trussed) and cover liberally with crushed sea salt or fine salt. Put it directly on a rack and place a roasting tray beneath to catch any moisture. Roast a 2kg bird, which is easily enough for 3–4 people, for 1 hour and 20 minutes. If you're worried about undercooking, don't be. Cook less rather than more. We can cook a bird more if it's undercooked but we can't recover from overcooking – even for a 2.5kg+ bird, don't roast for more than 1½ hours; for a 1.5kg, bird I'd only reduce this by 10 minutes. If you have a probe thermometer, at the end of the roasting time it should read 63–68°C* (which will rise as you leave it out) in the thick part of the breast and more in the leg. If you don't have a thermometer, feel the breast – it should be firm to the touch – and prod the inside leg with the tip of a knife or a skewer. If the meat isn't translucent anywhere, it's cooked.

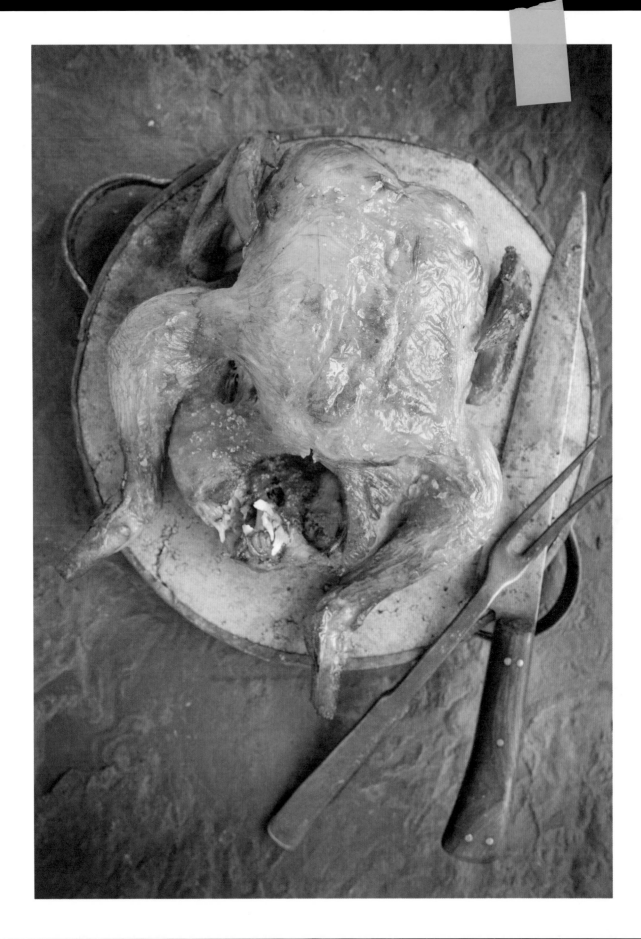

Slutty chicken continued

*For me this cooking temperature is perfect. If you want to stick firmly to health and safety guidelines, give it another 10 minutes or until it reaches an internal temperature of 73.9°C. I cook it for less time at home because it tastes better, but it's up to you how you cook it.

STEP 2: COOL
Take the bird out of the oven and leave on the worktop for 45–50 minutes, uncovered. This will cool the bird down enough to give us a chance to cook it at a high heat without drying it out.

STEP 3: BROWN AND CRISP
Turn the oven up to 220–250°C. When it's at temperature, put the bird back in and roast for 10 minutes to achieve a crispy skin. This timing is the same for pretty much any size of chicken. Remember the core temp has already been reached and the bird is cooked, so there is no need to check the internal temp. All we're doing here is getting a great finish and crispy skin.

Another, even better but slower method is at Step 2 to chill the bird overnight in the fridge. The next day, just before you plan to eat, set your oven to 220–250°C with a roasting tray inside and get a pan hot on the hob. Take the breasts off the carcass (being careful to keep the skin intact) and remove the legs. Flatten the breasts slightly by pressing them with a heavy pan to get a uniform thickness. Place the legs in the hot tray in the oven to roast for 15 minutes, whilst you fry the breasts, skin side down, in the pan with a touch of oil, pressing them down like a steak. Once the breasts are warmed through, which will take about 10 minutes, flip and baste with unsalted butter added to the pan, then cook for a couple more minutes. The skin on the breasts will be like glass and the flesh still juicy and moist. This method is a little trickier technically but the result tastes unbelievably good.

Roast potato crispy duck

1.5-2KG BIRD, SERVES 4-6

The main difference between chicken and duck is the thickness of the skin and the amount of fat. This means that the time needed to cook the skin is longer and the time taken to dry out the skin is much longer. Ducks are tricky to get right.

The Chinese have perfected a method for Peking Duck, which has a long drying-out process that involves hanging it, sometimes for days, in a dry environment. It's a complicated process – even more than some of mine – so I'm going to avoid it.

The other thing about Peking Duck, as well as Chinese variants such as Crispy Duck, is that the breast and legs are cooked through almost to incineration. There is nothing wrong with this as duck has a higher fat content than chicken, which means it won't dry out when overcooked. That said, when duck is cooked to a nice medium (57–63°C breast core temperature) rather than well-done, you get something that in my mind is on another level entirely.

Be warned: this is a two-day job, minimum. If you buy your duck a few days in advance, give it a heavy sprinkle of salt, cover with clingfilm and keep it in the fridge. Then start with the cooking of the skin, which for me is best done in water or oil as you will then get a direct cook.

Water is a hell of a lot safer than oil and less hassle. The water will start cooking the skin instantly so you don't need to cook it for such a long time. This process starts to break down the connective tissue in the skin. A duck roasted this way will serve 4–6.

STEP 1: POACH

Score the skin lightly with a sharp knife to penetrate to the fat but not much more. Score one way in 2cm intervals then at right angles the same way. I say right angles and 2cm, but in reality just score it as much as you like and don't bother with how it looks. Place the duck upside down in a pan or flameproof casserole big enough to hold the bird, and deep enough so you can fill the pan with cold water to come at least halfway up the duck. Set the pan on the heat and bring to the boil, then simmer for 15 minutes (if you have a thermometer, you're taking this up to no more than 60°C). Immediately transfer the pan to the sink and run cold water into the pan until the hot water is cold and the duck has cooled down enough to handle. Season with salt and place in the fridge till cold (overnight is best).

STEP 2: OVEN-DRY

Set the oven to 180°C, then set the duck on a rack on a roasting tray to catch any fat. Place in the oven to roast for 25 minutes. During this time we are drying out the skin and cooking out the

Roast potato crispy duck continued

connective proteins in it even further. If you have a probe thermometer, you're taking the breast up to no more than 60°C at its core.

STEP 3: FRIDGE-DRY AND COOL
Remove the duck from the oven and leave to cool for 20 minutes, then chill in the fridge for at least 24 hours, uncovered. The longer the duck spends in the fridge, the better as the fridge air will continue to dry out the skin.

STEP 4: BROWN AND CRISP
Set your oven to 220–250°C. Roast the duck straight from the fridge, on a rack with a roasting tray to catch any fat, for 15 minutes for medium (57–63°C on a probe thermometer) or 20 minutes for medium-well (64–69°C). Leave to cool down for 20 minutes at room temperature before serving.

If you want well-done Peking-style duck, roast for 30 minutes, then switch off the oven and leave the duck inside for a further 15 minutes or until fully crispy and sexy-looking.

Chicken-wing poussin

500G BIRD, SERVES 1

There is a tendency for people to give me a funny look when I teach them this method. Then they realise I'm Scottish and it's more a look of sympathy. When they taste it, they change their minds altogether.

Deep-fat frying is not the devil's work. It's pretty much the same as shallow-frying, but as the contact is instant and encompasses the entire surface area without turning or flipping, it's ideal for poultry and game. If you had a big enough fryer, I'd even recommend it for chicken and duck.

This same method can be used for almost all small game birds. With those such as pigeon and grouse, simply halve the slow-cook times to get a nice rare to medium-rare.

STEP 1: SLOW-COOK

A 500g poussin is enough for one person. Heat your oven to 125°C. Season the bird (slutty, not trussed) well, then place in the oven on a rack with a tray to catch any fat to cook for 35 minutes. This will fully cook the bird but we will have no crispy skin.

STEP 2: CHILL AND DRY

Remove the poussin from the oven. Cool for at least 30 minutes at room temperature, then chill in the fridge for 1 hour.

STEP 3: DEEP-FRY

Heat some vegetable oil in your deep-fat fryer to 180°C.

Deep-fry the poussin from fridge-cold for 6 minutes or until the skin is nice and crispy. As it comes out, hit it with a little more salt, drain and enjoy. Poussin may be a little pink around the legs, which is natural with smaller birds as they run around a lot and so produce more myoglobin. This is not an indication that it is undercooked. Translucent flesh is the only real indicator.

Twice-cooked pork belly

1.4KG BELLY, SERVES 4-6

To get perfect crackling on a pork belly is tough. You can't just slow-roast it. The skin might go hard and blister and look like great crackling, but only pieces of this will be crunchy – it will still have a chew in places. The idea behind the technique here is to focus on the skin first whilst being careful at all times not to overcook the meat (for me, pork belly, like pork ribs, should still have a little bite). In order to get the best crackling, some chefs cook the life out of the pork, leaving something that has lost its structure and most of the pork flavour. In order to do both skin and meat successfully, we have to break up the cooking into smaller steps.

Ask your butcher for a rolled belly joint no bigger that 10–12cm wide (the length doesn't really matter) – timings given here are for a 1.4kg belly (8–10cm wide) to serve 4–6 – and to make it as even as possible. Tell him not to score the skin. It's quite easy to prepare the belly yourself at home, tying up the joint with those blue elastic butcher's string loops that you just slide on. If you do this, you can use the Pork Cure recipe on page 121. Because of the lengthy processes here, you don't really have to pre-cure the belly as the time it takes to do the whole recipe is long enough. But it won't hurt.

STEP 1: POACH

Place the rolled belly in a pan and cover with cold water. Bring to the boil, then simmer for 20 minutes. Remove from the heat and leave to cool in the water for 20 minutes. The pork should reach an internal temperature of around 63°C (if it goes higher, don't worry – it can take an extra 20°C).

STEP 2: CHILL AND DRY

Place the pan in the sink and run cold water into the pan until the pork has cooled enough to handle. Lift it out and dry with a tea towel. Salt the skin, then leave in the fridge overnight, uncovered, to dry slightly and chill.

STEP 3: ROAST

Set your oven to 220°C. Roast the belly from fridge-cold for 1 hour, placing the belly on a rack with a tray to catch any fat underneath. The skin should puff up like a balloon. If it goes too dark, pull the belly out of the oven and turn down the temperature, then put it back in.

Thrice-cooked pork loin

1.5KG BONED AND ROLLED LOIN, SERVES 4-6

Start this recipe the day before you want to eat it. If this were for me, I'd knock a few minutes off these timings, but I don't want to get into trouble, so this recipe cooks the pork loin to medium. The big difference here is that loin can't be cooked as far as belly, so you have to reduce the end roasting time. But you add an extra low-oven drying time so the crackling cooks faster. Timings are for a 1.5kg (8–10cm) boned and rolled loin joint, which will serve 4–6 people.

STEP 1: POACH

Put the joint in a pan and cover with cold water. Bring to the boil, then simmer for 15 minutes. Remove from the heat and leave to cool in the water for 15 minutes. The pork should reach an internal temperature of around 55°C.

STEP 2: CHILL AND DRY

Place the pan in the sink under running cold water. When the pork has cooled down so it can be handled, lift it out and dry with a tea towel. Salt the skin, then leave in the fridge overnight, uncovered, to dry slightly and chill.

STEP 3: DRY-BAKE

Set your oven to 140°C. Cook the loin from fridge-cold for 40 minutes. On a probe thermometer it should read no more than 60°C internally.

STEP 4: CHILL

Remove the pork from the oven. Cool slightly, then leave it in the freezer for 2–3 hours, or overnight in the fridge, to chill completely.

STEP 5: ROAST

Set your oven to 220°C. Roast the pork from fridge-cold for 30 minutes, placing the meat on a rack with a tray to catch any fat underneath. The skin should puff up like a balloon. If it goes too dark, pull the pork out and turn down the temperature, then put it back in. The final internal temperature should be no higher than 63°C – if it's lower, don't worry as the core temp has already been reached during the previous cooking stages.

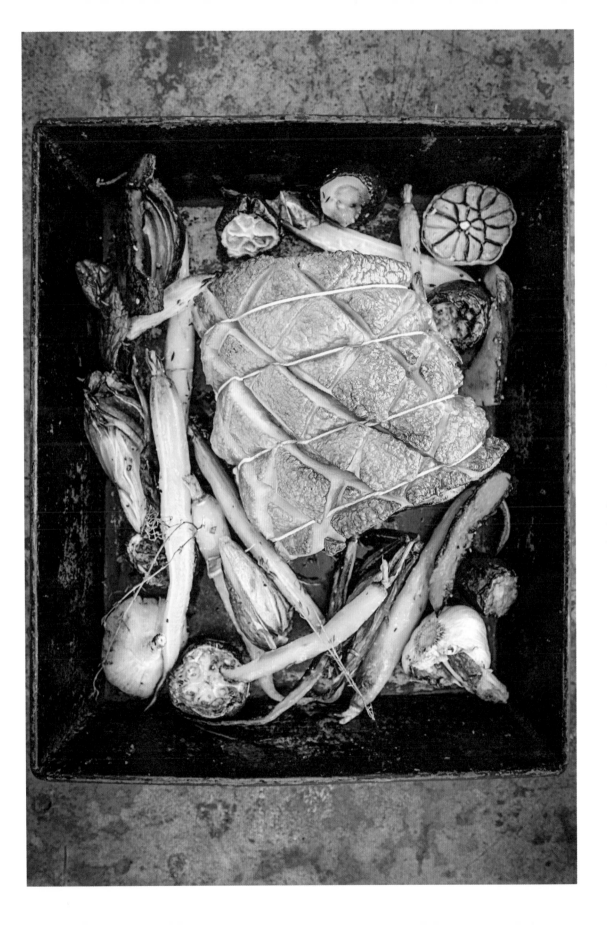

Rib roast on the bone

3-4 KG, SERVES 5-8

This is a large two- to three-bone joint with the ribcap left on. A 3–4kg rib roast will serve 5–8 people. I'm not a fan of cooking on the bone, but there really is nothing more impressive than pulling this bad boy out at a dinner party. The theatre of the joint itself justifies the reduced browning potential and heat distribution. In other words, it looks cool so who cares?

STEP 1: PAN-ROAST/SEAR

Set your oven to 120°C with a roasting tray inside and place a pan on a medium-high heat (you need a pan that will just hold the joint). This process will get really smoky, so turn on your extractor fan to high.

Start, from fridge-cold (although it hardly matters as it would take years to get this joint to room temp), by rendering the fat layer above the ribcap – place the joint face down in the hot pan. Then you can sear the beef in its own fat. Try to colour all over on each side as much as possible, pushing down the meat to get maximum contact with the hot pan, although the sheer weight of the joint should do this for you. Once the meat is coloured and is hot enough to melt the salt, season it with crushed sea salt. This searing process should take no more than 10 minutes.

STEP 2: SLOW-COOK

Place the joint, bone down, on the hot roasting tray in the oven and cook for:

- 1 hour 40 minutes for rare (40–47°C).
- 2 hours for medium-rare (48–56°C).
- 2 hours 20 minutes for medium (57–63°C).

My preference is medium-rare. As with any oven cooking, the central core temperature when you pull out the beef might be just under 50°C and the outer core (if it was an onion, the outer core would be the last three to four layers) just above 50°C. After 10 minutes out of the oven, the heat will be distributed by self-cooking to 50°C core temperature and the outside will cool to 50°C, making it even throughout.

STEP 3: SELF-COOK

Leave on the worktop, uncovered, for 20 minutes to self-cook and then cool down a little, which will make it easier to handle and carve. Slice the meat off the bone and cut into thick 1cm slices. Season the inside meat with a little crushed salt. You can pour the fat and juices in the pan/tray over the meat to get an extra boost in flavour and moisture.

Beef topside/rolled sirloin/ boneless rolled leg of lamb/ pork rib eye

2 - 2.5KG, SERVES 4 - 6

I have lumped these four cuts together because they are pretty much the same thing. Same dimensions – essentially a large cylindrical roasting joint – and same cooking times. A joint weighing 2–2.5kg (20–25cm thick) will serve 4–6 people. For topside, ask your butcher to tie it with a strip of fat on the top. I would suggest cooking the sirloin to rare, the topside and the lamb leg to medium-rare and the pork rib eye to medium.

Pork rib eye is probably the least well known of these cuts but it's one of my favourite roasting joints. It comes from carving the meat from under the shoulder blade in the pork butt. You can also slice this into pork shoulder steaks.

STEP 1: PAN-ROAST/SEAR

Set your oven to 120°C with a roasting tray inside and place a pan on a medium-high heat (you need a pan that will just hold the joint with a bit of room to move). This process will get really smoky, so turn on your extractor fan to high. Start by rendering the fat (if the joint has any) in the hot pan; if it has no fat, use a little vegetable oil at the start. Then try to get as much colour all over as possible, turning the joint slowly inch by inch. Don't forget the two ends need some pan love too. Once you've seared the meat, season it with crushed sea salt. The whole searing process should take no more than 10 minutes.

STEP 2: SLOW-COOK

Transfer the joint to a hot roasting tray. Place in the oven and cook for:
- 40 minutes for rare (40–47°C).
- 1 hour for medium-rare (48–56°C).
- 1 hour 20 minutes for medium (57–63°C).

STEP 3: SELF-COOK

Remove the joint from the oven. Leave on the worktop for 20 minutes, uncovered, to self-cook and cool a little, then slice the meat and season.

Lamb shoulder on the bone

2-2.5KG, SERVES 4-6

Lamb shoulder is great for a Sunday roast or any day of the week, and this is probably the most straightforward recipe imaginable. It's easy to tell when the lamb is done as it pulls itself off the bone so the bone begins to expose itself. The timings here are for a 2–2.5kg joint to serve 4–6 people. You can use the same method and timings for mutton or goat shoulder. Keep any leftovers and use to make some Lebanese-style wraps with minted yoghurt, lettuce and harissa.

STEP 1: SLOW-COOK

Set your oven to 120°C. Place the lamb in a roasting tray and splash a little water in the bottom – a tray with a raised rack is ideal. Season the flesh heavily with sea salt. Place in the oven and cook for 5 hours. The meat should pull away from the bone relatively easily but not without some effort – we still want a little texture and bite. The internal temperature will be 90°C or above, although this is more about feel than temperature. For some people, the lamb is ready to eat at this stage.

STEP 2: COOL

Remove the lamb from the oven. Spoon all the fat drippings from the bottom of the tray and use to baste the meat. Leave on the worktop for 1 hour or until cooled to 60°C. During this time, continue to spoon the fat over the surface, rubbing it in. As the fat cools you'll be spreading it rather than basting it.

STEP 3: ROAST

Set your oven to 250°C. When it reaches temperature, place the lamb back in the oven and roast for 10 minutes to give it some extra colour and finish it off. Once cooked, you can serve it as is on a big platter, or pull the meat off the bone – if you do this, make sure you pull it into the fat collected in the tray. Pulled meat has no fat and collagen surrounding it to prevent it from drying out, so you have to replace that with another fat.

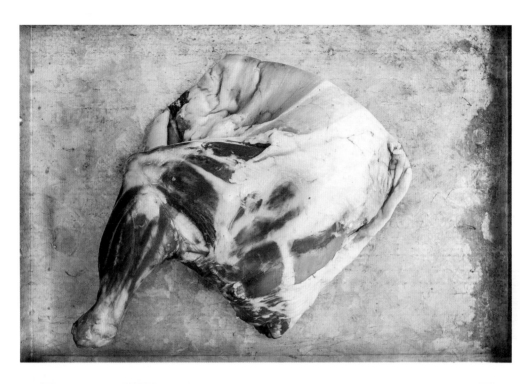

STOCKS, GRAVIES AND SIDE DISHES FOR ROASTS

Low-and-slow chicken stock

For this basic recipe, the most important thing is to find the right container. Stock can be made in a saucepan on the stove but this massively limits quantity and quality, as few households possess pans big enough. Instead we're going to oven-cook in a large, deep roasting tray or casserole with a lid for a period of at least 8 hours – but, most conveniently, overnight.

The other difference between this stock and any other recipe out there is the lack of vegetables and herbs and all that stuff. I like purity of product. Vegetable stock profiles can be added at a later stage or made separately. I don't think they're necessary. Chicken stock should be chicken stock. Vegetables bring little to the party.

A great tip is to reduce your stock right down and freeze it in ice-cube trays for later use. These can then easily be brought back to a bigger batch by simply thawing and adding water.

About 1kg chicken wings
    (or enough to ¾ fill
    your container)
Cold water
Maldon salt

Set your oven to 160°C. Spread out your chicken wings on a large baking tray and roast for 20 minutes. (If you are making a white stock, skip this browning step.) You can skim off any fat at this stage; pass it through a sieve and keep it in the fridge as it's great for cooking.

Transfer the wings to your deep roasting tray or casserole. Pour in cold water to cover and add a pinch of salt. Set the lid on top. To prevent too much evaporation, cover the lid first tightly with clingfilm and then with foil. (If you're using a roasting tray, cover it tightly with foil.)

Turn down your oven to 125°C. Place the container in the oven and leave to cook overnight or for at least 8 hours.

Remove from the oven. Strain the stock into a bowl, then cool and chill in the fridge. Once chilled, scrape off any fat that has risen to the top. If you want a more intense flavour, simply boil the stock to reduce to the right strength.

Low-and-slow pork stock

Use the same method as for Low-and-slow Chicken Stock (see page 117), but instead of chicken wings use 1kg mixed pork bones plus 2 pig's trotters.

Low-and-slow beef stock

Use the same method as for Low-and-slow Chicken Stock (see page 117), but instead of chicken wings use veal bones (if you can find them) or young cow bones – preferably from the shin or knuckle, although any will do in theory.

Basic gravy or jus

MAKES ABOUT 1 LITRE

2 large onions, sliced
Vegetable oil, for frying
1 carrot, diced
1 celery stick, diced
½ leek, diced
2 litres chicken or beef
    stock
500ml red wine
500ml Madeira
100ml brandy
3 bay leaves (break the
    leaves to release more
    flavour)
2 thyme sprigs
4 black peppercorns
4 garlic cloves, crushed
Maldon salt

Start by caramelising the onions in a little oil in a deep saucepan, adding a small pinch of salt early on. Once they have a deep colour, remove the onions from the pan. Add the other vegetables to the pan and sweat down until they start to colour too, then add the onions back in. Pour in the stock and reduce down by half (skim as the stock is coming to the boil and then as often as you can).

Now add the rest of the ingredients and keep simmering until you have the desired consistency. Strain through a fine sieve. If you're not serving straight away, you can keep this gravy in the fridge for up to a week, or longer if you freeze it.

Extra flavour

You can boost the flavour a level by adding the juices from the roasting tray. Or, if you have any spare bones and trimmings, roast these off in a pan, then deglaze all the sticky bits at the bottom with a little water or wine; add all this and the bones to the stock before reducing.

Fish sauce gravy

This might sound a little odd but it's worth a try. Make the Basic Gravy as above but add some fish sauce and tomato ketchup at the end to give the gravy a huge umami boost. A couple of teaspoons of each per litre is probably enough.

Duck offal jus

MAKES ABOUT 1 LITRE

I like to eat this with peanut butter on toast, but I'm not recommending it as it's a bit weird.

2 duck carcasses, chopped
    in half or quartered
2 litres chicken stock
1 litre cold water
2 duck necks
3 duck gizzards, trimmed
2 large onions, sliced
1 carrot, diced
1 celery stick, diced
½ leek, diced
500ml red wine
200ml port
100ml brandy
3 bay leaves (break the
    leaves to release more
    flavour)
2 thyme sprigs
4 black peppercorns
4 garlic cloves, crushed
2 duck livers
2 duck hearts
Maldon salt

Heat the oven to 160°C, then roast off your carcasses for 30 minutes. Transfer to a large pan or pot (leave the oven on) and pour in the chicken stock and water. Bring to the boil, then simmer for about 1 hour or until you have 2 litres of duck stock. Strain and reserve.

Whilst the stock is simmering, put the necks and gizzards in a flameproof roasting/baking tray and roast for 30 minutes or until you get a good colour. Remove the necks and gizzards and set aside.

Set the tray over a medium heat. Add all the vegetables to the tray and scrape up the brown sticky bits from the bottom. Deglaze with the strained duck stock, then bring to the boil and reduce by half. Add the remaining ingredients, except the duck livers, hearts, necks and gizzards. Simmer until reduced almost to a thick sauce.

Meanwhile, remove the meat from the necks and chop up the gizzards. Also chop up the livers and hearts.

Once the sauce is ready and still hot, add all the duck meat and offal. Transfer to a blender or food processor and blitz until smooth, or use a hand-held blender in the pan. Season with salt. If the jus is too thick, add a little water. Serve.

Pork cure

MAKES ENOUGH FOR 2-3 BELLIES

Use this on a pork belly before roasting (see page 104).

40g fennel seeds
10g garlic salt
5 bay leaves
10g cracked black
    peppercorns
10 juniper berries
150g Maldon sea salt
Chopped parsley
Finely chopped garlic
Grated lemon zest

Put the fennel seeds, garlic salt, bay leaves, peppercorns and juniper berries in a spice mill or blender and blitz to a coarse mix. Add the salt and mix well.

Sprinkle evenly over the pork on the flesh side, then add a light sprinkling of chopped parsley, garlic and lemon zest (the amount of each of these is up to you – it's not an exact science). If you want, you can roll up the pork now, but this cure can also be used for an unrolled belly.

Duck glaze

MAKES ENOUGH FOR 2-3 DUCKS

100g apricot jam
100g cranberry jelly
50ml soy sauce
5 teaspoons rice wine
    vinegar
½ teaspoon ginger paste
½ teaspoon garlic paste
1 teaspoon five-spice
    powder
1 fresh green chilli

Blitz everything together in a blender or food processor until smooth.

Once your crispy duck is cooked (see pages 99–101), brush the glaze mixture all over, then give the duck a blast in a hot oven or under a hot grill for 2–3 minutes to glaze it. Or just serve the glaze on the side as a sauce.

Sourdough, Marmite and butter bread sauce

MAKES ABOUT 400ML, SERVES 4-5

This is not the traditional recipe where you spike the onion with the cloves and all that jazz. Never much saw the point of that myself. Also, I use sourdough, which has more flavour than straight white bread, and a small dollop of Marmite to give a yeasty boost. And I use way more butter than normal because, well, who doesn't like butter?

½ loaf of sourdough bread
75g unsalted butter
Vegetable oil, for frying
1 onion, sliced
1 clove
1 bay leaf (break the leaf to release more flavour)
3 pinches nutmeg
350ml whole milk
50ml double cream
1 teaspoon Marmite (or more if you dig it)
Maldon salt and black pepper

Set your oven to 100°C. Cut the crusts off the sourdough and reserve, then cut the bread into cubes. Spread the cubes on a baking tray and dry them out a little in the oven, then pulse in a blender or food processor to make breadcrumbs. You want about 150g of breadcrumbs for this recipe.

Heat 25g of the butter with a little oil in a saucepan and add your onion with a tiny pinch of salt. Sweat for a few minutes until the onion starts to develop a gentle colour, then add the clove, bay leaf and nutmeg. Let the spices cook out a little until you get a nice aroma filling the room. Add your bread crusts (they're full of flavour) and then the milk. Bring to the boil. Remove from the heat, cover and leave to infuse for 1–2 hours (or 30 minutes if you're impatient).

Strain the milk and get it back on the heat. Stir in the breadcrumbs and cook on a low heat until they swell and the sauce thickens. Cube up the rest of your butter and add very slowly, one cube at a time, until you have incorporated every last bit, stirring as you go.

Finish with the cream, Marmite and a seasoning of salt and pepper. Serve almost immediately.

Burnt bread sauce

Cut the loaf into thick slices (leave the crusts on if you like, they add extra flavour) and toast until the bread is slightly burnt but still with some bounce to it. Blitz it up into breadcrumbs, then continue with the recipe as above.

Mint and roasted garlic sauce

SERVES 4 - 6

1 garlic bulb
Vegetable oil, for drizzling
2 tablespoons chopped mint
1 tablespoon chopped
    parsley
1 tablespoon caster sugar
100ml boiling water
About 100ml white wine
    vinegar
Maldon salt

Set your oven to 180°C. Slice the garlic bulb across in half, drizzle with a little oil and wrap in foil. Roast for 30–40 minutes. Leave to cool.

In a bowl, mix the chopped herbs with the sugar and the peeled cloves of your roasted garlic. Add the boiling water. Stir and mash up the garlic more, then leave to cool.

Once cool, stir in vinegar to taste and season with salt. Serve.

Boozy apple sauce

SERVES 10

I find apple sauce a little too sweet most of the time and I like booze, so this recipe is just right for me. It doesn't use cooking apples so is super super quick to make.

50g unsalted butter
50g light soft brown sugar
5 apples (good-quality dessert/eating, not cooking), peeled, cored and cut into small dice
2 teaspoons bourbon whiskey
2 teaspoons Madeira
1 teaspoon white wine vinegar

Melt the butter and sugar in a saucepan until bubbling and looking like caramel. Add the diced apples and toss until they are coated, then cook until soft but not squishy. Tip into a bowl.

Strain the juice from the apples back into the pan; reserve the apples. Return the pan to the heat and add the bourbon, Madeira and vinegar. Reduce by half.

Add to the apples and blitz until smooth. If the resulting sauce is too watery, put it back in the pan and cook a little more. If it's too thick, add a little water. Serve.

Horseradish butter sauce

MAKES ABOUT 400ML, SERVES 4-6

Horseradish cream sauce is all fine and good but my biggest problem is it's never as good as the shop-bought stuff. The main problem for me is that the cream sucks the life out of the horseradish so the sauce is never punchy enough. So instead of cream, I use butter and wine.

100ml white wine
2 tablespoons white wine
    vinegar
1 bay leaf (break the leaf
    to release more flavour)
1 thyme sprig
50ml double cream
250g unsalted butter, cubed
About 100g fresh
    horseradish, peeled
Juice of ½ lemon
Maldon salt and black
    pepper

Reduce the white wine and vinegar with the herbs to a trickle, then add the cream and reduce a little more. Remove the herbs and take the pan off the heat.

Add the butter, lump by lump, stirring, until it's fully incorporated. As you do this, keep the sauce warm by putting the pan back on the heat now and again. Season with salt and pepper.

Grate in as much horseradish as your palate can handle and finish with the lemon juice. Serve.

Lamb fat and garlic toast

SERVES 4 – 6

Lamb fat good, fried toast good, garlic good. Voilà!

At least 100g lamb fat
50g unsalted butter, cubed,
    plus extra to finish
4 thick slices of white bread
2 garlic cloves, peeled and
    left whole
2 teaspoons chopped
    parsley
Maldon salt and black
    pepper

To render the lamb fat, put it in a saucepan with a little water on a low heat. Once the fat has melted, pass through a sieve to remove any solids. Pour 50g of the rendered fat back into the pan. On a low heat, slowly add the butter, a cube at a time, waiting for each to melt and emulsify before adding the next, swirling the pan and stirring the butter in as you go. Season with salt to taste, then cool and chill in the fridge to set.

Spread some lamb butter on both sides of each slice of bread, then fry in a dry frying pan until crisp on both sides. Finish with more butter to melt in.

Rub one side of the toast with the garlic and sprinkle with parsley and black pepper. Serve.

Roast potatoes

Some say the heart and soul of any Sunday roast is the Yorkshire pudding. For me it's the roast potatoes. They're fluffy, salty and light in the middle, crunchy and golden on the outside. You can never make too many and the next day you can smash them up and cook them in a hash (see page 78) or add to a salad, or even make another roast, which is never a bad option.

However many potatoes you want to eat (Maris piper or any other dry-matter spud will do)
About 100ml white wine vinegar
Oil or rendered beef dripping/duck fat – in fact, any fat
Garlic cloves, crushed
Thyme sprigs
Rosemary sprigs
Maldon salt

Peel your potatoes and cut them into pieces the size of a golf ball. Take a fork and scrape the edges. Go mad on this – you want lots of texture. Place the potatoes in a pan of cold water, which you have salted to taste like the sea. Add the vinegar a drop at a time. You want to just be able to taste it.

Bring to the boil and simmer for 2–5 minutes, then take off the heat and leave the potatoes to cool in the water. Once they are almost falling apart, pour into a colander to drain. Shake it about to fluff up the edges of the potato pieces even more. Leave to cool at room temperature for about 30 minutes.

Set your oven to 160°C and pour a thin layer of oil or fat into a roasting tray. Place in the oven to heat. Once the fat is smoking, remove from the oven and toss your potatoes in the fat, then add some crushed garlic and herbs. Roast for about 35 minutes or until the potatoes have just started to colour.

Remove from the oven and cool in the tray for 30 minutes, rolling the potatoes around in the fat now and again, and maybe gently crushing them a little too.

Turn your oven up to 220°C. When you are about ready to serve the potatoes, give them a final blast in the hot oven for 5–10 minutes to crisp up.

Beef-dripping Yorkshires

MAKES 4-6, DEPENDING ON SIZE

Why people wait until they have a roast dinner to make these is beyond me. I'd eat them every day if I could: stuff them with cold cuts of meat for lunch; spread them with jam or Nutella for breakfast; use them instead of pitta bread for a kebab; or just eat them by themselves with some gravy or sauce to dip into. Size isn't everything – for me the larger you make them, the less of the soft gooey texture you get, which I prefer to the airy crisp effect of a huge one. Somewhere in the middle is just right but it's all down to personal taste, like anything.

100ml plain flour
100ml eggs
75ml milk
5 teaspoons double cream
200ml rendered aged
    beef dripping
Maldon salt

Use a measuring jug to measure out all the ingredients by volume, not by weight. Start with the flour and transfer it to a bowl, then measure your eggs, followed by the milk and cream. Mix until smooth – a few lumps add some interest, so don't be clinical. Leave the batter out at room temperature for an hour or so, or in the fridge overnight.

Set your oven to 200°C. Add some salt to the batter. Put a decent amount of fat in each cup of a muffin tray, then heat in the oven.

When the fat is hot, open the oven door and pour the batter into the muffin cups. The more generous you are, the bigger the puddings will be.

Bake for about 20 minutes or until risen and golden. Turn off your oven and leave the puddings inside for another 5 minutes – this will help them to keep height and not droop – then serve.

Bone-marrow cauliflower cheese

SERVES 4-6

2 cauliflowers, leaves removed

Vegetable oil, for drizzling

3 garlic cloves, 2 crushed and 1 finely sliced

2 thyme sprigs

1 rosemary sprig, plus chopped rosemary to finish

50g Parmesan cheese

50g bone marrow (out of the bone)

50g unsalted butter

65g plain flour

300ml hot milk

300g Westcombe Cheddar (or any strong Cheddar), grated

½ teaspoon English mustard

Maldon salt and cayenne pepper

Set your oven to 180°C and put a baking tray in to heat.

Slice the cauliflowers in half lengthways, then cut each half in half again lengthways. Lay these quarters on the hot baking tray. Drizzle over some oil, add some salt and cayenne, and toss to coat. Add the crushed garlic and herb sprigs to the tray and toss again. Roast the cauliflower for 30–40 minutes until soft. As soon as you take the tray out of the oven, grate the Parmesan all over the cauliflower, then transfer to a hot serving dish.

Whilst the cauliflower is roasting, make the sauce. Melt the bone marrow in a pan. Pass through a sieve to remove any nasty bits, then put the marrow back in the cleaned pan. Add the butter and sliced garlic. When melted, stir in the flour. Cook out the flour for 3–4 minutes, stirring, to make a roux, then slowly stir in the hot milk and bring to the boil to thicken. Finish with the grated Cheddar, mustard, and salt and cayenne to taste.

Pour the sauce over the cauliflower to cover and sprinkle with a little cayenne and chopped rosemary to finish.

Seasonal roast veg

Sunday roasts needn't be all about parsnips and carrots, lovely though they are. This isn't so much a recipe, more a process of using what's seasonal and a bit different. Along with a little meat, some roast potatoes and a dash of gravy, you're flying with a great meal, with minimum hassle.

*Veg to consider if you're
    bored with parsnips
    and carrots:*
Fennel
Leeks
Aubergines
Butternut squash
Courgettes
Beetroots
Jerusalem artichokes
Turnips
Asparagus
Globe artichokes
Portobello mushrooms
Calcots or big salad onions
Tropea onions or red
    onions
Shallots
Peppers
Whole heads garlic

FOR ROASTING
Vegetable oil
Garlic cloves, crushed
Herb sprigs
Maldon salt

The method for cooking almost all of these is pretty much the same. It's really all about timing and size, which can be bypassed by slicing all the tougher/harder vegetables into small pieces and leaving the softest veg whole or in big pieces. Then you can cook them all together. If a few of the veg are still a bit hard when you take them out, you can separate them and give them a little more time in the oven.

Set your oven to 180–200°C and get a roasting tray hot. Peel the veg and slice/chop as necessary. Put the prepared veg in the hot tray and drizzle liberally with oil. Add some crushed garlic, a few choice herbs and some salt. Roast for about 30 minutes, tossing everything every 10 minutes.

Pancetta and onion hash cakes

SERVES 10

Bored with roast potatoes? Then try these. They're basically potatoes with meat inside. (If you get bored with these, we're done.) You can substitute fried bacon or any braised meat for the pancetta or any herb for the sage, or add other cooked vegetables. The cakes are great for breakfast with a poached egg too.

4 large Maris Piper
   potatoes (or similar
   dry-matter spuds)
1 onion, sliced
Vegetable oil, for frying
150g pancetta, diced
3 sage leaves, finely
   chopped
Maldon salt and black
   pepper

Cook the potatoes in a pan of boiling, salted water for about 30 minutes or until the skin pulls back from the flesh. The spuds should still be a bit hard in the middle to keep their starch, which is what's going to stick these cakes together without using a binding agent. Drain.

Whilst still a little hot, peel the potatoes and coarsely grate on a box grater into thick strands. If you've cooked them right they should still be a bit sticky. Set aside in a bowl.

Turn your oven on to 180°C. Fry the onion in a little oil until nicely caramelised, then add to the potatoes with the pancetta and sage. Season to taste and mix everything together. Shape the mixture into burger-like patties by hand or using a mould.

Heat some oil in an ovenproof frying pan and fry the cakes to get a golden brown colour on both sides. Transfer to the oven to finish cooking for about 5 minutes.

Moroccan butter-roasted heritage carrots

SERVES 4-6

Every time I see heritage carrots I wonder why we settled on orange. There are other varieties that are beautifully shaded purple, yellow, white or a deep red. Even in their raw state they brighten up my day. Here we simply pan-roast the carrots in butter, then add a North African-style garnish. They are great with roast lamb or chicken.

10 mixed heritage carrots (about 1kg)

100g unsalted butter, cut into cubes

2 teaspoons ras el hanout, plus extra to finish

1 tablespoon chopped dill, plus extra to finish

1 tablespoon chopped parsley

2 teaspoons toasted sesame seeds

1 tablespoon toasted pine nuts

Maldon salt

FOR THE SAUCE

50ml soured cream

1 preserved lemon

15g tahini

2 garlic cloves, peeled and left whole

Juice of ½ lemon

Cut the carrots in half lengthways or into quarters if they're big. Make sure the pieces are all the same size.

Put the carrots in a frying pan on a low heat and add the butter, cube by cube. The pan should be hot but take care not to burn the butter (it should be foaming). Keep the carrots frying in the butter until they're just tender, turning and spooning the butter over them as they are cooking. If the butter starts to burn, add a little water to the pan to cool it down. Season with salt and the ras el hanout and set aside.

Whilst the carrots are cooking, make the sauce. Put the soured cream, whole preserved lemon, tahini, garlic and lemon juice in a blender or food processor and blitz until smooth.

Add the herbs, sesame seeds and pine nuts to the carrots with a little of the sauce and toss together. Top with the rest of the sauce and finish with extra dill and a sprinkle of ras el hanout.

Spiced red cabbage and fennel with ginger wine

SERVES 6-8

Take this nice and slow for the best results.

1 large red cabbage, cored
    and finely chopped
1 fennel bulb, finely
    chopped
1 dessert/eating apple,
    peeled, cored and grated
1 red onion, finely chopped
50g unsalted butter
1 cinnamon stick
¼ teaspoon ground
    star anise
¼ teaspoon grated nutmeg
50ml red wine vinegar
100ml ginger wine
100ml cold water
Maldon salt and black
    pepper

Mix together the cabbage, fennel, apple and onion with a few pinches of salt, then let them all sit in a colander for 30 minutes.

Melt the butter in a saucepan, add the spices and cook a little, then add the cabbage mix and sweat it down until starting to soften.

Next add the vinegar, ginger wine and water and bring to the boil. Simmer until everything is cooked down and the liquid is almost evaporated.

Season to taste and add more vinegar, if necessary.

Chargrilled Szechuan Hispi cabbage

SERVES 4 - 6

Chargrilled Hispi cabbage is simple to make and great on its own, but some Szechuan pepper gives it a pleasing tingle.

15g Maldon sea salt
15g Szechuan pepper
4 Hispi cabbages
Vegetable oil, for brushing
100g unsalted butter

Blitz the salt and Szechuan pepper together in a spice grinder to make a powder.

Remove the outer leaves from the cabbages, then cut each in half through the core. Blanch in lightly salted water for about 5 minutes or until soft. Place in iced water to cool, then drain.

Get a ridged griddle pan nice and hot, or prepare a BBQ. Brush the cabbage halves with a little oil, then grill until you have a nice char all over.

Season with the salt mix and serve with a dollop of butter on top of each half.

Crushed beef-dripping potatoes fridge buffet

SERVES 4-6

This is less a recipe and more a way to serve great fridge leftovers. You can add almost anything to this – leftover charcuterie, any cooked vegetable, pickles, cheese, herbs or the leftovers from a Sunday dinner. Just pick the foods you like and throw them in. It's similar to those garbage plates you get in American burger joints these days but a little more refined.

500g new potatoes
50g rendered aged beef
   dripping
10 good-quality tinned
   brown anchovy fillets,
   drained
60g goat's cheese, cut into
   1cm slices
15 cornichons, roughly
   chopped
Handful of parsley,
   chopped
2 teaspoons chopped
   marjoram
Juice of 1 lemon
Maldon salt and black
   pepper

Put the potatoes in a pan of cold salty water and bring to the boil. After boiling for a minute or two, remove from the heat and let the potatoes self-cook for 10 minutes or so until they feel soft.

Drain the potatoes, then crush them and leave to cool. This can all be done in advance or even the day before.

When you're getting ready to eat, turn your oven on to 180°C. Put the potatoes in a small roasting tray and cover with the rendered beef dripping. Scatter the anchovies, goat's cheese and cornichons over the potatoes, then bake for 10 minutes.

Add the herbs and lemon juice and season to taste. Serve with your meat of choice plus maybe a few Yorkshire puddings.

BRAISES

Braising is one of life's great cooking pleasures. To immerse a tough piece of meat in simmering water or other liquid and leave it for hours until it is so tender that it can be pulled apart, is not only satisfying from the eating side, but also gives the extra bonus of a stock you can use to make a sauce. In this section, we also look at developing a fat from the cooking method. So you will be left with all the tools you need to create almost any braised meat dish, whether it's a stew, a pie, a pasta sauce, a filling or any of the vast array of interesting, flavourful side dishes.

The overnight braise

The biggest drawback of low-and-slow cooking is obviously the time it takes. This isn't just a problem for the home cook; it's a problem in professional kitchens too. We don't have an infinite amount of space or ovens, and stocks and long braises take up room we need for service. We come home from work at maybe 6-7 o'clock and want to eat by 9. Even at the weekend how much time do we have to spend watching a pot? My suggestion is to cook it longer and get on with your day.

I call this an overnight braise because in the restaurant we do it overnight but really it can be done at anytime, even while we're at work, playing football, at the gym, out shopping or watching a whole series of *Game of Thrones*. It is a powerful tool in your cooking arsenal – an important answer to the problem of cooking proper food in our busy lives.

The first questions people ask when you suggest unsupervised cooking are: 'What if my house burns down?', 'What if the meat overcooks and I'm not there?' and 'I don't want braised meat for breakfast, are you mental?' We hate not being able to keep a watchful eye.

Unless you are really, really unlucky, your house will not burn down. Your oven won't magically become more likely to burst into flames at night. If it ever looks like it might do this, put down this book and buy a new oven.

Remember too that you're braising at low temperatures, so the meat almost cannot overcook. And if you're braising overnight, you can't sneak a peek into the oven by opening the door and losing the heat, thus possibly cocking things up.

A braising timeline

Season, then colour your piece of meat in a pan. You don't need to go crazy. The more colour the better but if it's an awkwardly shaped piece of meat, colour what you can and concentrate on the fatty bits which develop better flavours. What we're looking for here is to develop the browning flavours to flavour the stock.

Place the meat in a (tight fitting) roasting tray or casserole and pour over the cold braising liquid. Cover with a paper cartouche (see page 261). If you have an old gas oven with exposed flames a lid placed ajar is safer.

Turn your oven on and put the tray or pot into the oven.

Cook at 120°C for 4 hours
Cook at 110°C for 6–7 hours
Cook at 105°C for 9–11 hours
Cook at 100°C for 12–15 hours

NOTE: These are pretty exact timings and the temperature does matter a great deal. I would recommend checking your oven temperature first. I lived in two flats writing this book and the second oven I used was as much as 20°C out which here is about a 5 hour mistake. If you don't have a thermometer then do a trial run first before leaving it alone.

Remove the tray or pot from the oven. Lift out the meat and strain the stock into another container. Leave it whole or break up the meat (don't shred it, you want large chunks) and moisten with a little of the stock to prevent it from drying out. Leave to cool and either use it now or for an even better braised meat place both the meat and stock in the fridge and leave it over night.

Have you ever realised a takeaway curry tastes better the next day? That's why I suggest doing this.

Cooking without a lid

Braising is actually direct cooking, but using lower temperatures. When we cook indirectly the temperature is half of the oven temperature on the surface until the centre reaches equilibrium. In a deep enough braise however we cook the water indirectly, but the meat is directly cooked by the water. So for a 120°C cooker the meat cooks at 60°C, but for a sealed braise it cooks at 100°C because the water reaches boiling point. Cooking without a lid might seem counter-productive, but an interesting thing happens at low temperatures in a humid environment.

Much like 'the stall' in the BBQ section (see page 186), when we cook at low temperatures and the water is allowed to evaporate, this uses a lot of energy. This in turn means it never reaches boiling point and instead holds at a low simmering temperature for quite some time, which is perfect for braising. (My perfect sous vide temperature for tough meats is around 83°C and this method gives similar results). This is due to the evaporation of the water at low temperatures keeping the temperature low or 'evaporating cooking'. If we were to seal the braise, we could negate some or all evaporation, but we would be cooking at a higher temperature over the duration as the water would reach near boiling point, which for slow cooking is quite a high and fast temperature. Its like setting a smoker to 200°C. Evaporation happens on the surface of the water so if the surface area is minimised, less evaporation will occur. Placing a cartouche made from greaseproof paper or baking parchment on the surface of the liquid helps to minimise the surface area, as does using a narrower tray or pot. If you are left with insufficient braising stock for the final recipe, simply top it up with water.

The result

You'll have meat that is cooked perfectly tender and a stock to make a sauce. The low braising temperature will create a better stock than one made by traditional methods. In addition, you'll have the rendered fat that will float to the top of the stock as it chills, which can be used in the recipe or to cook something else.

Now you can simply reheat all or part of the braise for lunch or dinner that day or the next, or any other day of the week. Your meal will take minutes, not hours. This is restaurant thinking that home cooks can benefit from. A number of other dishes can be prepared ahead this way, including soups and roast dinners.

Braising stock

With the overnight method and a large piece of meat, you can start with plain water because slow cooking will turn it into a good stock as it cooks slowly and never hits a rolling boil. But you could add some chicken stock or any other leftover stock, which will help boost the flavour of the dish. A 50/50 ratio of stock to water is good. Leftover vegetables such as leek greens, carrots, onion and celery trimmings and garlic can also be added but don't buy them specially. For stocks Get the meaty gelatinous properties in first then, when making a sauce, I add the vegetables and extra flavour components.

Bolognaise sauce/ragù

SERVES 6-8

Mix this with your favourite pasta or use in a lasagne. It can also be served as a stew.

FOR THE BRAISE
1 smoked ham hock
Vegetable oil
500g beef chuck
2 veal cheeks
Enough water/stock to
　　cover, approx. 1-2 litres
　　(see Braising Stock,
　　page 147)

FOR THE SAUCE
3 garlic cloves, thickly
　　sliced
2 carrots, finely diced
2 celery sticks, finely diced
2 onions, finely diced
150g tomato paste
400ml red wine
100ml Madeira
2 bay leaves (break the
　　leaves to release more
　　flavour)
1 rosemary sprig
Maldon salt and black
　　pepper

Start by blanching the hock three times to get rid of excess salt: put it in a pan of cold water, bring to the boil, drain and rinse. Repeat with fresh cold water each time.

Get a frying pan hot on the stovetop with a little oil and colour the whole ham hock, beef chuck and veal cheeks in small batches. Once you're done colouring, deglaze the pan with a little water, stock or red wine and reserve with the meat.

Set the oven to 100°C. Transfer the meat and juices to a suitable, tight-fitting container. Pour in the water/stock. Cover with a cartouche (see page 261) but no lid and leave to braise for 12-15 hours (or use other times/temperatures on page 146).

Lift the meats out of the pot. Whilst still warm, break up the meat without shredding it, discarding any bones from the hock. Drizzle over some of the braising stock to keep the meat moist. Leave to cool. Cover with clingfilm and keep in the fridge until needed. Keep the stock in the fridge too. Once chilled, skim any fat from the surface of the stock and reserve.

When you're ready to make the sauce, heat a little of the skimmed-off fat in a saucepan. If you don't have any fat, vegetable oil or butter will do. Throw in the garlic and cook over a medium heat until it starts to get colour. Then add the carrots, celery and onions with a little salt and cook until soft.

Add the tomato paste next, turn up the heat and cook, stirring occasionally, until the mix turns a dark red. Add all the rest of the sauce ingredients along with the braising stock and cook down until reduced to a good consistency.

Stir in all the meat and continue cooking until you have your desired consistency. Season to taste. I like to serve this with a generous sprinkling of Parmesan.

Beef shin stovies

SERVES 4-6

A Scottish classic, this is usually made from the leftovers of a Sunday roast. Here instead I've use beef shin in an overnight braise to create a side dish to rival all other sides.

Vegetable oil
2kg beef shin (preferably whole but thick-cut leg steaks will do)
2 litres of water/stock (see Braising Stock, page 147)
3 onions, finely sliced
3 bay leaves (break the leaves to release more flavour)
Few thyme sprigs
4 garlic cloves, crushed
1kg Maris Piper potatoes, peeled and cut into 2cm-thick chunks
2 tablespoons chopped parsley
Maldon salt and black pepper

Get a frying pan hot on the stovetop with a little oil and colour your meat as best you can. Once you're done colouring, deglaze the pan with a little water, stock or red wine and reserve with the meat.

Set the oven to 100°C. Transfer the meat and juices to a suitable container. Pour in the water/stock. Cover with a cartouche (see page 261) but no lid and leave to braise in the oven for 12-15 hours (or use other times/temperatures on page 146).

Lift the meat out of the pot. Whilst still warm, pick the meat off the bone and drizzle over some of the braising stock to keep the meat moist. Leave to cool. Cover with clingfilm or foil and keep in the fridge until needed. Put the stock in the fridge too. Once chilled, skim any fat from the surface of the stock and reserve. If you have more than 2 litres of braising stock, boil to reduce it to this quantity.

Heat a little of the skimmed-off fat (or vegetable oil if you have no fat) in a saucepan and deeply caramelise the onions with a pinch of salt. Then add the stock, the bay, thyme, garlic and potatoes. Simmer until the potatoes are tender. If the stock is too thin at this point, remove the potatoes and reduce the stock to a thick soup consistency, then add back the potatoes. Discard the bay and thyme.

Add the braised meat and mix gently. When hot, season and sprinkle with the parsley to garnish.

Goat shoulder tagine

SERVES 4-6

Goat is heaven-sent meat for slow braising. If you can't get it, mutton or lamb make good substitutes. Serve this with some spiced couscous or fluffy white rice.

1 x 2kg kid goat shoulder or belly (on the bone)
Enough water/stock to cover, approx. 1-2 litres (see Braising Stock, page 147)
10 dried apricots
100g raisins
300ml white wine
1 onion, sliced
1 tablespoon ras el hanout
1 red pepper, deseeded and sliced
1 tablespoon tomato paste
2 teaspoons harissa
300g tinned tomatoes
3 garlic cloves, crushed
100g cooked or tinned chickpeas
1 tablespoon runny honey
2 tablespoons chopped coriander
2 tablespoons chopped parsley
Maldon salt and black pepper

Get a frying pan hot on the stovetop with a little oil and colour your meat. Once you're done colouring, deglaze the pan with a little water, stock or red wine and reserve with the meat.

Turn the oven to 100°C. Transfer the meat and juices to a suitable, tight-fitting container. Pour in the water/stock. Cover with a cartouche (see page 261) but no lid and leave to braise for 12-15 hours (or use other times/temperatures on page 146). At the same time, soak the apricots and raisins in the white wine overnight.

Lift the meat out of the pot. Whilst still warm, pick the meat off the bone and drizzle some of the braising stock over the meat to keep it moist. Leave to cool. Cover with clingfilm and keep in the fridge until needed. Put the stock in the fridge too. Once chilled, skim any fat from the surface of the stock and reserve. If you have more than 500ml of stock, boil to reduce it to this quantity.

Heat some of the skimmed-off fat in a pan or flameproof casserole and cook the onion with a little salt and the ras el hanout until tender. Add the red pepper and cook a little longer, then stir in the tomato paste and harissa and cook to a deep red colour.

Next add the apricots and raisins with their soaking wine. Bring to the boil and boil for about 2 minutes. Add the goat stock, the tinned tomatoes and garlic. Bring back to the boil, then cook down until reduced by two-thirds and beginning to thicken.

Stir in all the goat meat and continue cooking until you have the desired consistency. Mix in the chickpeas and honey, then season and finish with the chopped fresh herbs.

Ox cheek sausage rolls

MAKES 6

Whether you're having a dinner party, feeding your kids or a hungry sofa monster, these are the real deal. Enjoy with brown sauce or your favourite hot sauce.

Vegetable oil, for frying
3 ox cheeks
Enough water/stock to cover, approx. 1-2 litres (see Braising Stock, page 147)
200ml red wine
1 bay leaf (break the leaf to release more flavour)
2 garlic cloves
1 teaspoon English mustard, or to taste
1 teaspoon chopped parsley
1 teaspoon picked thyme leaves
2 sheets of all-butter puff pastry, thawed if frozen
3 egg yolks, beaten

Get a frying pan hot on the stovetop with a little oil and colour the cheeks in batches. Once you're done colouring, deglaze the pan with a little water, stock or red wine and reserve with the meat.

Set the oven to 100°C. Transfer the meat to a suitable tight fitting container. Pour in the water/stock. Cover with a cartouche (see page 261) but no lid and leave to braise for 12-15 hours (or use other times/temperatures on page 146).

Lift the cheeks out of the pot. Drizzle over some of the braising stock to keep them moist, then cool, cover with clingfilm and keep in the fridge until needed. Put the stock in the fridge too. Once chilled, skim any fat from the surface of the stock.

When you're ready to make the rolls, turn on your oven again to 180°C.

Reduce the braising stock to 500ml, then add the wine, bay leaf and garlic cloves. Boil to reduce to a thick sticky jus. Discard the bay and garlic, then stir in the mustard to taste and finish with the herbs. Keep the jus warm, or chill and reheat when needed.

Slice the cold ox cheeks into long batons 2.5cm thick. Unroll one of the pastry sheets on the worktop and lay half of the ox cheek batons in a line down the middle. Brush the edges of the pastry with a little beaten egg yolk, then roll the pastry over to make a long sausage roll. Transfer to a baking tray lined with baking parchment. Repeat with the remaining sheet of pastry and ox cheek.

Brush the pastry with more beaten egg yolk, then bake for 15 minutes or until puffed up and golden brown.

Slice each roll across into three portions. Serve hot, with the jus to dip into for extra pleasure.

Pig's head and ham hock pork pie

SERVES 8-10

I have to admit that this is tough to make but it is a good pie, much better than one of those stupid puff-top pies without a bottom. It's extreme blind-baking but the bacon adds just enough moisture to keep the crust from going dry during the long bake. You can fill the crust with any braised meat and gravy, although the pork and ham mixture here is good and savoury.

FOR THE FILLING

1 smoked ham hock
1 boned pig's head
Enough water/stock to cover, approx. 1-2 litres (see Braising Stock page 147)
100g unsalted butter, melted
2 garlic cloves, finely chopped
1 tablespoon chopped parsley
1 teaspoon grated lemon zest
Maldon salt and pepper

FOR THE HOT-WATER CRUST

6 streaky bacon rashers
475g plain flour, plus extra for dusting
100g cold unsalted butter
125ml cold water
75g lard
½ teaspoon Maldon salt
400g polenta
1 egg, beaten, for glazing

Start by blanching the hock three times to get rid of excess salt: put it in a pan of cold water, bring to the boil, drain and rinse. Repeat with fresh cold water each time.

Get a frying pan hot on the stovetop with a little oil and colour the ham hock and then the pig's head. Once you're done colouring, deglaze the pan with a little water, stock or red wine and reserve with the meat.

Turn the oven to 100°C. Transfer the meat and juices to a suitable tight fitting container. Pour in the water/stock. Cover with a cartouche (see page 261) but no lid and leave to braise for 12-15 hours (or use other times/temperatures on page 146).

Lift the meat out of the pot. Whilst still warm, pick apart the meat and fat, discarding any skin and bones but keeping the fat. Add the butter, garlic, parsley and lemon zest to the meat and season with salt to taste. Cover and keep in the fridge until needed. Keep the stock in the fridge too. Once chilled, skim any fat from the surface of the stock.

Now you can make the pie crust. Set your oven to 180°C. First, roll out the bacon rashers between two sheets of greaseproof paper until as thin as possible. Set aside.

Sift the flour into a bowl and rub in the butter until the mix looks like breadcrumbs. Put the water and lard in a pan and bring to the boil. When boiling and the lard has melted, add to the flour with the salt. Bring together into a dough.

Chill the dough in the fridge for about 5 minutes.

Pig's head and ham hock pork pie continued

Roll out the dough away from you on a lightly floured worktop to make a rectangle. Fold the top down and the bottom up to meet in the centre, then fold over in half like a book. Repeat this rolling out and folding twice.

Cut off a third of the dough for the lid and set aside wrapped in clingfilm. Roll out the rest to a 30cm round. Use to line a deep 20cm cake tin with a loose base, like a springform tin. Lay the bacon rashers over the bottom and up the sides to cover as much of the pastry case as possible, letting the ends of the rashers hang over the edge.

Lay a large sheet of clingfilm over the bacon, smoothing it out and into the corners of the pastry case. There should be plenty of clingfilm left hanging over the rim of the tin. Fill the clingfilm-lined pastry case with the polenta. Fold the edges of the clingfilm back over the top and then the ends of the bacon. (The polenta and bacon are removed and not eaten, but if you are concerned about using clingfilm, please use baking parchment instead.)

Roll out the reserved dough to make a lid. Press it on top of the pastry case, using a little water to seal the edges together, crimping the edges as you go. Cut a 2.5cm hole in the centre of the lid, then brush all over with beaten egg. Bake for 30–40 minutes or until golden brown. Cool on a wire rack.

Once cold enough, pour out the polenta through the hole in the lid and pick out the clingfilm/parchment and bacon lining. If a little polenta or bacon lingers, it's no big deal. If it's clingfilm it's a bigger deal, so get all of it out.

Warm the braised meat filling in a covered shallow tray in a low oven – you need the butter and fat to be loose so it will be easier to fill the pie. Warm the stock too so that it is liquid.

Fill the pastry case with the braised meat, pushing it through the hole in the lid with your fingers, to the sides too, until the case is packed. Add the stock through the hole, then leave to set at room temperature. Remove the pie from the tin. The pie is best served when the filling has just set, but it can be kept in the fridge and enjoyed all week.

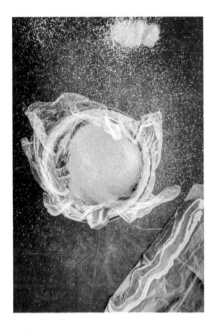  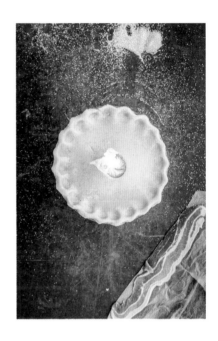

Lamb belly steamed pudding

MAKES 1 PUDDING (SERVES 4-6)

Steamed pudding is a British classic. The lamb belly element adds a richness to the dish and the shank gives it body.

1 lamb belly/breast (on the bone)
1 lamb shank
3 fresh lambs kidneys
Enough water/stock to cover, approx. 1-2 litres (see Braising Stock, page 147)
3 onions, sliced
1 teaspoon fennel seeds
1 teaspoon cumin seeds
100ml white wine
100ml Madeira
3 garlic cloves, lightly smashed
2 bay leaves (break the leaves to release more flavour)
1 tablespoon chopped mint
1 tablespoon chopped parsley
Maldon salt and black pepper

FOR THE PASTRY
350g self-raising flour, plus extra for dusting
175g shredded suet
about 300ml cold water
50g soft unsalted butter for the basins

Get a frying pan hot on the stovetop with a little oil and colour the lamb belly/breast then the shank and then the kidneys. Once you're done colouring, deglaze the pan with a little water, stock or red wine and reserve with the meat.

Turn the oven to 100°C. Transfer the belly/breast and shank (but not the kidneys) and juices to a suitable, tight-fitting container. Pour in the water/stock. Cover with a cartouche (see page 261) but no lid and leave to braise for 12-15 hours (or use the other times/temperatures on page 146).

Lift the belly and shank out of the pot. Whilst still warm, pick the meat off the bone in thick chunks. Drizzle some of the braising stock over the meat to keep it moist, then cool, cover with clingfilm and keep in the fridge until needed along with the stock. Once chilled, skim any fat from the surface of the stock and reserve.

Heat some of the skimmed-off lamb fat in a pan, add the onions and cook to a deep brown. Add the spices and toast for a minute, then add the wine, Madeira, garlic, bay leaves and braising stock. Bring to the boil and reduce by a quarter.

Pour half of this into another pan and cook down to a sauce-like glaze to use as an extra jus.

Cook the rest in the first pan until almost thick, then add the lamb. Continue to cook this until the liquid is almost all evaporated but the meat is still moist. Discard the bay leaves and garlic, add the mint and parsley, and season to taste.

Add the browned kidneys to the meat filling, mix in then set the meat mixture and jus aside.

To make the pastry, sift the flour into a bowl with a

Lamb belly steamed pudding continued

pinch of salt and gently stir in the suet. Add the water and bring together to form a soft dough. Wrap in clingfilm and leave to rest for 30 minutes.

Butter a 2-pint (1.2 litre) pudding basin.

Roll out the pastry on a floured worktop to make a 25cm round that's about 1cm thick. Cut out a quarter of this round to make the lid.

Line the basin with the remaining pastry round and press down to fit.

Roll out the reserved quarter to make a lid.

Add the meat filling then top with the lid, using water to stick the edges together.

Place a piece of baking parchment on top of a sheet of foil (both larger than the top of the pudding basin) and make a large pleat in the middle, folding both sheets together. Place this pleated cover foil-side up on top of the basin and secure it with string or a rubber band. Cut off any excess foil/paper that hangs below the string/band.

Steam the puddings for 1½ hours.

Turn out to serve. Reheat the jus then pour over the pudding for extra richness.

Duck neck and cep tortellini with sage butter sauce

SERVES 4

Duck necks are cheap, ceps are not. You can use another wild mushroom, but the combination of ceps with duck is stunning. All you need is a simple sauce to make this the perfect dinner. If you can't be bothered to make pasta dough, those ready-made wonton wraps you can buy are almost as good. (See recipe photos overleaf.)

FOR THE FILLING
Vegetable oil, for frying
6 duck necks
Enough water/stock to cover, approx. 1-2 litres (see Braising Stock, page 147)
1 onion, sliced
3 juniper berries
5 fennel seeds
100ml white wine
100ml Madeira
2 bay leaves (break the leaves to release more flavour)
2 thyme sprigs
3 garlic cloves, crushed
2 fresh ceps (about 200g)
Unsalted butter, for frying
2 sage leaves, finely chopped

Get a frying pan hot on the stovetop with a little oil and colour your duck necks. Once you're done colouring, deglaze the pan with a little water, stock or wine and reserve with the meat.

Turn the oven to 100°C. Transfer the meat and juices to a suitable, tight-fitting container. Pour in the water/stock. Cover with a cartouche (see page 261) but no lid and leave to braise for 12-15 hours (or use other times/temperatures on page 146).

Lift the necks out of the pot. Whilst still warm, pick the meat from the bones. Drizzle over some of the braising stock to keep the meat moist. Leave to cool. Cover with clingfilm and keep in the fridge until needed. Keep the stock in the fridge too. Once chilled, skim any fat from the surface of the stock and reserve.

Heat some of the skimmed-off fat in a pan, add the onion and cook until coloured. Add the juniper berries and fennel seeds and cook a little longer, then add the wine, Madeira, bay leaves, thyme, garlic and stock. Bring to the boil and reduce almost to a glaze, then add the duck meat and cook a bit longer. Cool, then keep in the fridge until needed.

Meanwhile, chop up your ceps into small cubes and fry in a little butter until just cooked and nicely coloured. Add the sage and season to taste.

FOR THE PASTA DOUGH
2 eggs
200g '00' pasta flour, plus
    extra for dusting

FOR THE SAUCE
50g unsalted butter
4 sage leaves
½ lemon
Maldon salt and black
    pepper

Cool and chill, then mix with the duck meat.

Now make your pasta dough. Combine the eggs and flour in a food processor and blitz to make a dough, adding a little cold water if necessary. Knead the dough for 2–3 minutes, then shape into a ball, wrap in clingfilm and leave in the fridge for 30 minutes.

Flour your worktop. Flatten out the dough with a rolling pin, then pass through a floured pasta machine – start at the thickest setting and gradually reduce with each rolling until you reach the thinnest setting.

Cut the sheet of dough into 10cm squares. Place a ball of duck filling the size of a thumb tip in the centre of each square. Wet the edges with water or beaten egg and fold a point to its opposite point to create a triangle. Then fold the two outer points in, one on top of the other, sticking them together with a little more water or egg. Repeat to make as many tortellini as possible. Dust the tortellini with flour or semolina so they don't stick to each other and keep in the fridge until needed.

When you are ready to cook the tortellini, bring a large pot of water to the boil. Add salt, then cook the tortellini, in batches, for 2–3 minutes, draining each batch briefly on kitchen paper.

Meanwhile, make the sauce. Heat the butter in a frying pan or saucepan until it turns hazelnut brown. Add the sage leaves and cook for a little longer, then finish with the lemon juice and add salt to taste. Pour the sauce over the hot tortellini once on the plates.

Mutton rolls

SERVES 8 - 10

Here's a Sri Lankan-inspired dish with a few twists. You can effectively use any braised meat for this and any spice combo. It's a block of deep-fried meat. How can you lose?

1 whole mutton shoulder
(about 2kg)
Enough water/stock to
cover, approx. 1-2
litres (see Braising Stock,
page 147)
2 onions, sliced
2 teaspoons garam masala
2 fresh red chillies, finely
sliced
2 teaspoons finely chopped
garlic
2 teaspoons finely chopped
fresh ginger
1 teaspoon grated lemon
zest
1 tablespoon chopped
parsley
Maldon salt and black
pepper

TO COAT AND COOK
2 eggs
100ml milk
100g plain flour
200g panko breadcrumbs
Oil, for deep-frying

Get a frying pan hot on the stovetop and colour your meat. Once you're done colouring, deglaze the pan with a little water, stock or red wine and reserve with the meat.

Turn the oven to 100°C. Transfer the meat and juices to a suitable, tight-fitting container. Pour in the water/stock. Cover with a cartouche (see page 261) but no lid and leave to braise for 12-15 hours (or use the other times/temperatures on page 146).

Lift the shoulder out of the pot. Whilst still warm, pick the meat from the bones. Drizzle over some of the braising stock to keep the meat moist. Leave to cool. Cover with clingfilm and keep in the fridge until needed. Keep the stock in the fridge too. Once chilled, skim any fat from the surface of the stock and reserve.

Heat some of the skimmed-off fat in a pan and cook the onions until soft. Stir in the garam masala and cook for a little longer. Add the stock, bring to the boil and reduce until almost a glaze. Add the meat and cook until most of the liquid has evaporated. Mix in the chillies, garlic, ginger, lemon zest and parsley. Season to taste, then leave to cool slightly.

Lay a sheet of clingfilm on the worktop and spoon some meat across in a sausage shape (about 5cm thick). Fold the clingfilm over the meat and roll into a tight sausage. Twist the ends tightly and tie with string. Repeat until you run out of meat. Chill for at least 4 hours to set.

Mix the eggs and milk in a shallow dish. Spread the flour on a tray or plate and the panko breadcrumbs on another. Remove the clingfilm and slice the sausages into 10cm lengths. Dip first in flour, then in egg and then in panko. Repeat this coating twice. Chill if not frying straight away.

Heat some oil in a deep-fat fryer or deep pan to 180°C and set your oven to 160°C. Deep-fry the mutton rolls, in batches, for about 4 minutes or until coloured all over. Drain on kitchen paper, then spread them out on a baking tray and finish cooking in the oven for 8–10 minutes. Serve hot with your favourite chilli sauce.

Chicken noodle soup

SERVES 4

Warm and comforting, this is what to eat when you're feeling down and need a chicken soup hug. It's also great for hangovers (which might be the same thing). Feel free to add extra accessories or delete any – crispy garlic, coriander leaves, pulled chicken breast meat, soft-boiled eggs or anything else you can think off. Also use any noodle you like – rice, egg, ramen or whatever. They're all good.

2kg chicken wings

4 litres cold water/chicken stock (see Braising Stock, page 147)

300g minced chicken thigh

Soy sauce, to taste

Toasted sesame oil, to taste

2 onions, sliced

1 carrot, roughly chopped

3 garlic cloves, crushed

2 teaspoons sriracha (hot chilli sauce), plus more for serving

Vegetable oil, for frying

200g chicken skin (should be available from your butcher; if not, take all the skin off 2 birds)

250g dried egg noodles

3 spring onions, finely sliced

2 fresh red chillies, finely sliced

Maldon salt

Set the oven to 100°C. Place the chicken wings in a casserole or roasting tray. Pour in the water/stock. Cover with a cartouche (see page 261) but no lid and leave to braise in the oven for 12-15 hours (or use other times/temperatures on page 146).

Strain the chicken stock into a bowl, cool and chill (discard the wings). Once chilled, skim off any fat that has risen to the top and reserve.

Mix 50–100g of the skimmed-off fat with the chicken mince. Season with soy sauce and sesame oil. Roll into mini meatballs and chill.

Melt the rest of the skimmed-off fat in a saucepan, add the onions and cook with a pinch of salt until soft. Add the carrot and garlic and cook for a few more minutes, then stir in the sriracha and cook until the mixture is a deep reddish-brown. Pour in the chicken stock, bring to the boil then reduce until you have the flavour you want. Skim off any foam that comes to the surface.

Meanwhile, fry the meatballs in a little oil in a frying pan until lightly browned all over and cooked through. Remove and reserve.

Finely chop up the chicken skin and fry in the pan until crisp. Remove and reserve also.

To finish, strain the soup and return to the pan. Bring back to the boil, then add the noodles and cook until just tender. Warm through the meatballs in the soup and season with soy and sesame oil to taste. Ladle the soup into bowls, sprinkle with sliced spring onions and chilli and the crispy skin. Serve with more sriracha on the side.

Lamb shoulder butter masala

SERVES 6 - 8

This can be used to make any Indian curry but butter masala is my favourite. Add extra chilli, if you're like me, and keep it saucy.

1 small lamb shoulder (about 2kg on the bone)
Enough water/stock to cover, approx. 1-2 litres (see Braising Stock, page 147)
4 onions, sliced
1 teaspoon chilli powder
¼ teaspoon ground turmeric
1 teaspoon garam masala
1 teaspoon dried fenugreek leaves
Seeds from 4 cardamom pods
1 teaspoon ginger paste
1 teaspoon garlic paste
2 teaspoons finely chopped fresh green chilli
2 tablespoons chopped coriander stalks
1 tablespoon ground almonds, mixed with a little water to a paste
½ teaspoon soft light brown sugar
1 tablespoon tomato paste
200g chopped tomatoes
100g unsalted butter
2 tablespoons single cream
2 tablespoons chopped coriander leaves
Finely sliced fresh green and red chillies, to garnish
Lime halves, to serve
Maldon salt and pepper

Get a frying pan hot on the stovetop and colour your meat. Once you're done colouring, deglaze the pan with a little water, stock or red wine and reserve with the meat.

Turn the oven to 100°C. Transfer the meat and juices to a suitable, tight-fitting container. Pour in the water/stock. Cover with a cartouche (see page 261) but no lid and leave to braise for 12-15 hours (or use other times/temperatures on page 146).

Lift the shoulder out of the pot. Whilst still warm, pull the meat from the bone. Drizzle over some of the braising stock to keep the meat moist. Cool, then cover with clingfilm and keep in the fridge until needed. Keep the stock in the fridge too. Once chilled, skim any fat from the surface of the stock and reserve.

Heat some of the skimmed-off fat in a pan, add the onions with a pinch of salt and cook until brown. Add all the spices and cook out, stirring occasionally, until the aroma hits you. Add the ginger and garlic pastes, the chopped chilli, coriander stalks, almond paste, sugar and tomato paste. Stir well, then cook for a few more minutes.

Pour in the tomatoes and the lamb stock. Bring to the boil and reduce by half. Blitz in a blender/food processor (or with a hand-held blender in the pan). Return to the pan and add the meat. Reheat the meat in the sauce, then remove it with a slotted spoon.

Stir the butter and cream into the sauce until emulsified and season to taste. Add the meat bit by bit. You want a loose buttery sauce – if you add a lot of meat, it will suck up too much moisture. (Any left over can be kept in the fridge for 3 days and used in a salad or a sandwich.) Garnish with the chopped coriander leaves and sliced chillies. Serve with basmati rice and lime.

Pork belly bo ssam

SERVES 4-6

This is a great way to get a family round the table. Korean food is all about family and sharing. If you have a Korean store near by, buy the tiny anchovies and simply fry them up with some garlic.

1 x 1.5kg thick end boneless pork belly

Enough water/stock to cover, approx. 1-2 litres (see Braising Stock, page 147)

2 tablespoons gochujang (Korean hot chilli paste)

1 tablespoon gochugaru (Korean chilli powder)

Toasted sesame oil, to taste

3 garlic cloves, thickly sliced

2 teaspoons black sesame seeds

1 spring onion, finely sliced

Maldon salt

FOR THE SSAM JANG KETCHUP

2 teaspoons doenjang (Korean fermented soya bean paste)

4 teaspoons gochujang (Korean hot chilli paste)

8 teaspoons tomato ketchup

FOR THE TEMPURA-FRIED ANCHOVIES

Oil for deep-frying

12 or more boquerones

Set the oven to 100°C. Place the meat in a casserole or roasting tray, skin-side down. Pour in the water/stock. Cover with a cartouche (see page 261) but no lid and leave to braise for 12-15 hours (or use other times/temperatures, page 146).

Lift the belly out of the pot and place in a container. Drizzle over some of the braising stock to keep the meat moist, then cool, cover with clingfilm and chill in the fridge. Once chilled, skim any fat from the surface of the stock and reserve.

Reduce the remaining stock until it's roughly 400ml, then stir in the chilli paste and powder, along with sesame oil to taste.

When the belly is cold, cut into slices 1cm thick and 10cm long. Keep in the fridge until needed.

Before serving, heat some of the skimmed-off fat in a frying pan and fry the garlic until lightly browned; remove and reserve. Season the belly slices with salt, then sear on both sides, getting a good colour. At the last minute, add a few spoonfuls of the stock and reduce to a sticky sauce to glaze the meat. Place on a serving plate and garnish with the sesame seeds, roasted garlic and spring onion.

To make the ketchup, blitz together all the ingredients in a blender or food processor until smooth. Transfer to a small serving bowl. Put the lettuce leaves and kimchi in serving bowls, and get the rice and Potato Bokkeum ready to serve.

For the anchovies, heat some oil in a deep-fat fryer or deep pan to 180°C. Mix the flour with enough cold

(Spanish marinated
  anchovy fillets)
100g tempura flour
Cold sparkling water

TO SERVE
6 baby Gem lettuces,
  separated into leaves
150g kimchi (store-bought
  or make your own – see
  note)
200g steamed white rice
100g Potato Bokkeum
  (see page 83)
Bottle(s) of soju (Korean
  booze)

sparkling water to make a thick batter. Dip the anchovies
in the batter and deep-fry for a few minutes until crispy.
Drain briefly on kitchen paper.

Eat by filling the lettuce leaves with the belly and any
mixture of the side dishes. Play about with different
fillings and drink lots of *soju* shots.

NOTE: To make kimchi, salt Chinese cabbage leaves
for 6 hours, then rinse and dry. Mix with kimchi paste
(see Kimchi Hollandaise, page 57) and leave in a sealed
sterilised jar in the fridge for at least a week before eating.

BBQ/ Slow-smoking

To me, barbecue/barbeque (BBQ) is a general term for cooking with fire and wood and the equipment we use to do it. It's slightly confusing because a lot of people have strong feelings about its origins and also the terminology surrounding it. I'm not interested in all that. The most important point to make is that there are two types of BBQ cooking: direct high-heat grilling, where we cook close to the heat source, and the indirect method, where we slow-cook or slow-smoke away from the heat source. When we compare these to the rest of this book, the grilling is actually the same as using the frying pan and the indirect cooking is exactly the same as using the oven.

In this chapter, I'll be dealing mainly with slow-smoking, which is an indirect BBQ method using wood in an enclosed space. If you don't have a BBQ/smoker, you could do most of these recipes in an oven instead, but the flavour of the smoke will, of course, be lacking.

I refer to the cooking temperature of the BBQ quite a lot and I'm assuming that your BBQ has a temperature gauge, as many do. If it doesn't, you could buy an oven thermometer and stick it inside; however, you'd need to keep opening and closing the lid to read it, so it's not 100 per cent ideal. Better is to use a probe thermometer with a wire, which you can get from any online BBQ store or catering shop. With this you can measure the temperature from outside the BBQ. You can even get ones that hook up to your mobile phone so you can check your BBQ cooking whilst you're in the pub.

From a terminology aspect (because it does get confusing) a smoker is a BBQ but a BBQ is not necessarily a smoker as it can be just a grill. The difference is that a BBQ grill doesn't provide an enclosed space for smoking food. Most common BBQs can be both, depending on whether you open or close the lid.

There are some people who consider direct grilling with a closed lid. This is possible if you cook directly above the coals but it's not really grilling. It's more like combining hot oven cooking and grilling. Meats will cook more quickly but the grill bars will not be as hot because the airflow is reduced. This leads to uneven cooking; a gassy, unpleasant taste from the high combustion in some cases; and increased moisture loss. Also we lose the advantage of flipping the meat often, as described in the Steak chapter (see page 35). Some manufacturers have got behind this idea of 'oven grilling', as it is faster and easier if you're not getting to grips with proper grilling. If only speed impresses you, then maybe this is your thing too.

How to light a BBQ

For any BBQ used for smoking the method for setting it up is the same. You want to light a small area only – coals are heat, so the fewer coals you light at once the easier it will be to control the heat. As you cook, the heat will move to another area and the area that was hot before will cool. This gives you longer smoking periods where you don't need to keep adding coals, and it won't get crazy hot.

Make sure the vents are open (1). I use a gas blowtorch (or you can use firelighters or some lit coals you've cooked on your gas stovetop), aiming it into a small area of the coals near the middle (2). Once five or six coals are glowing, I leave it for 5 minutes before closing the lid (3). Wait for the heat to reach the desired temperature, then add your wood (some onto the lit coals and some onto the unlit coals). Close up the vents to halfway (4). Put in the meat (5). After an hour, if the temperature drops, open the vents further; if it climbs, then close them up a little bit more.

For direct grilling, leave the lid off and open the vents wide (or halfway if it's a windy day). Light the coals in three or four places – don't add too much coal in the first place unless the grill bars are super thin and don't retain the heat.

If you have thin grill bars, you will need to cook off the heat of the coals rather than the heat retained in the bars, otherwise your meat will be grey and rather sad-looking. It's worth investing in some good thick grill bars as they make all the difference.

For both direct and indirect cooking, remember you can always add more coals. Heating up is easier than cooling down.

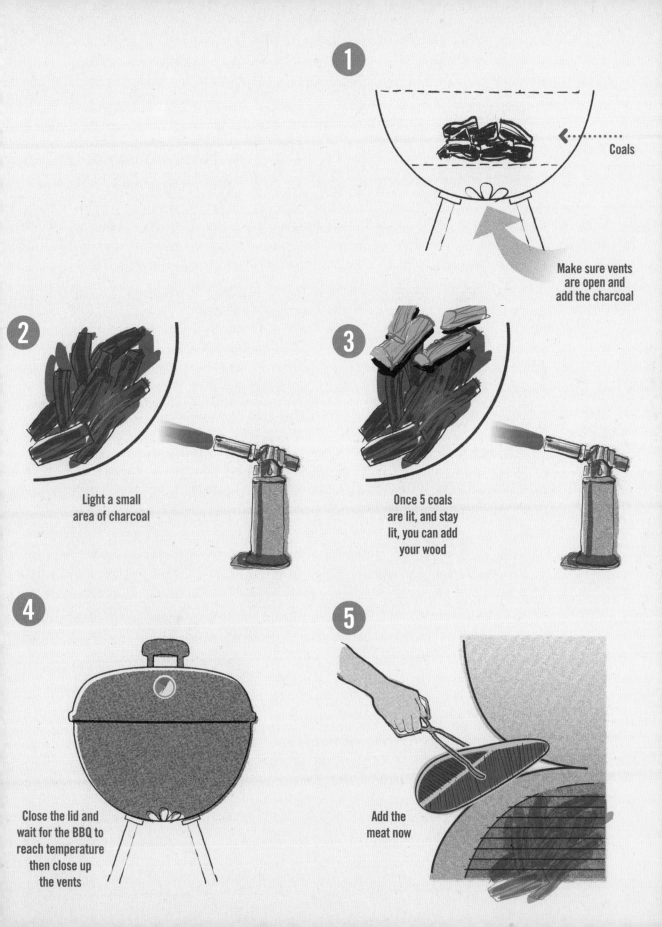

1

Coals

Make sure vents are open and add the charcoal

2

Light a small area of charcoal

3

Once 5 coals are lit, and stay lit, you can add your wood

4

Close the lid and wait for the BBQ to reach temperature then close up the vents

5

Add the meat now

What wood to use

The only real point of using wood in BBQ cooking is to layer the flavour of the woodsmoke on to your meat. So choosing the right wood to use is pretty fundamental. Unfortunately not doing this is a very common mistake.

First of all you need a hardwood. Softwoods like pine contain too much sap and burn too quickly and they can make your smoker taste nasty. You really want some good oak, hickory, beech, alder, walnut, sweet chestnut, mesquite or a fruit wood such as apple, pear or cherry. Buy wood that's been air-dried preferably, but definitely dried. If in doubt, buy from a wood specialist – this is not the thing to scrimp on when slow-smoking.

Buy the biggest chunks your smoker can accommodate. You get better combustion with larger pieces of wood, but then again don't go putting half a log inside a tiny kettle BBQ.

The ideal size of wood chunks for most medium-sized smokers is about that of a fist. These will burn slow and steady so you don't have to keep adding more for short cooks like chicken or pork ribs.

If you have to use wood chips, don't soak them first. If they're soaked, they'll just steam until they are dry – when you consider you want the smoke to hit the meat as early as possible, this is hugely counter-productive.

Instead, put the chips in two foil containers and poke holes in them, then place one on the hot coals and the other on the coals that have yet to be lit. One will light immediately and the other once the lit coals have spread. Chips are useful for foods that only need to smoke for a short amount of time, such as fish or small game. They produce high levels of smoke very quickly.

Smoke from wood should be clean and smell good. No matter what wood you use, you need only give it a quick sniff as it's burning to tell whether or not it's going to work for you. Also, if there is dirty black smoke you will know immediately that something isn't right. Use your eyes and your nose and you can't go far wrong.

Choosing charcoal

Charcoal is way more about heat than flavour. Whilst there is some flavour to be got from charcoal, it is subtle unless you are using super-high-quality coals. The advantage of briquettes is they burn more evenly and stay hotter for longer. I avoid cheap briquettes that contain chemicals – I don't want these anywhere near my food. Will you taste the chemicals? Probably not as much as you think, but why add them if they don't need to be there?

I mainly use good-quality local lumpwood charcoal. It's quick to light and it will last for most cooking in a decent smoker. You can buy this charcoal online as well as in good butcher's shops. The stuff you buy in the supermarket isn't terrible, but it's usually full of chemicals, is much less sustainable and gives a dirty smoke.

Wood or charcoal and wood?

You can cook with wood alone, and it will yield better results in terms of flavour than wood with charcoal, but you will need to keep adding more wood during the cooking as it burns down very quickly and will rapidly lose heat when it does. For home cooks, it's usually more convenient to build a charcoal fire to which you add

wood, as the charcoal will sustain an even heat for longer.

For very long, slow smokes, using charcoal with wood has its advantages. After 4–5 hours, if you've added enough wood, you will have smoked the food as much as you will ever need to. You can smoke it more, but you will need to keep adding moisture to the wood as the meat will start to dry up and smoke won't penetrate the crust around the meat. Also, if the wood isn't clean, you might over-smoke your food. It's a delicate balance and depends a lot on the type of wood you use. With a charcoal fire, you can effectively add as much wood as you like in the first 4–5 hours, then just stop and keep the charcoal fire going.

If you're a BBQ pro, I'd say learn this the hard way, but if you're only cooking now and again, charcoal fires are an effective cheat – they enable better results than if you keep messing up with all-wood fires.

Meat starting temperatures

I never bring meat to room temperature before barbecuing or smoking it – I place fridge-cold meat into the smoker. Being cold, it takes longer for the meat to crust up and, therefore, gives it more time to smoke.

The stall

When you cook large cuts of meat at low temperatures, for the first few hours the temperature rises as it should. But at around 73°C core temp, the upward curve flattens out and the meat stops cooking. At some points it actually cools down – this is the stall, and is caused by the moisture the meat is losing. That is cooling it down faster than the heat from the charcoal/

wood fire is raising the temperature. When we sweat, the same thing happens.

There are two ways to tackle the stall. One is to turn up the heat by opening the air vents. The other is to wrap the meat in foil or peach paper/butcher's paper, which reduces the moisture loss in the same way that braising or boiling does.

When people tell you about 20-hour smoked/barbecued meat, you might want to point out to them that a) their smoking/barbecuing temperature was way too low, and b) most of that time was spent losing moisture and making the meat drier, sitting at 70–74°C.

How hot should my smoker be?

Some pit masters cook hot and fast, which means at 140–150°C, whilst others cook really low at 100–120°C. I like to hover inbetween at 120–140°C, depending on the meat. Big, fatty meat cuts like beef ribs, ox cheek and pig's head can take higher heat than most, but in general for leaner pork, poultry and beef brisket, I tend to stay as close to 120°C as I can. Cooking too low means you spend more time stalling than you should, even on quick cooks, and cooking too high means you get less smoke during the cook.

Spraying meat and water pans

A lot of BBQ tipsters tell you to place a water pan in the smoker, or spray water or other liquid on to the meat whilst it's cooking. The theory behind this is sound, but for most meats I don't bother unless it's a long, slow cook. There are two reasons usually given for doing it. The first is that the humidity keeps the outside of the meat moist, which enables more smoke absorption. This is true although it

depends on the type of wood you're using. With strong woods like oak I don't think it's necessary, but with a lighter wood like apple it helps a great deal.

The other main reason is to add a weight to the smoke, which helps it linger a little longer and improves the smoke circulation. Think of it like clouds. Darker clouds that carry rainwater are lower in the atmosphere because they are denser. The same goes for smoke – you don't want your smoke simply flying out of your smoker. It needs time to sit with the meat.

Try it both ways – with a spray/water pan or without – and see for yourself. To spray, use some of the vinegar baste/mop on page 230 or plain water, or a mixture of the two, and load up a clean garden spray bottle. After the first few hours in the smoker, spray the meat once every hour. To use a water pan, simply place it in the smoker near the heat source and leave it to do its job uncovered.

Types of barbecues for smoking

All smokers (non-electric/gas) operate by the same general principles. A fire creates heat and smoke; the smoke is cooled slightly by travelling a certain distance before reaching the meat; the smoke moves past the meat and then out of a vent, which in some cases causes convection in the smoker.

There is usually a vent in and out at either end of the smoker – one vent near the heat source, which controls the oxygen levels to the fire and, in doing so, its temperature; and one vent at the other end, past where the meat is placed, which pulls the air through at different rates depending on how open or closed it is, thus affecting the temperature. These vents are usually adjustable in size so you can have some form of temperature control. Most smokers only differ in price due to their size and the quality of the insulation, which affects smoking times and efficiency.

Opposite are some of the most popular designs I recommend.

For long, slow smoking I'd suggest buying the thickest and best BBQ/smoker you can afford. If you're barbecuing the odd chicken or sausages once a year, a cheap kettle is fine and will yield great results.

Smokers are best used outside – or inside with minimal ventilation. The reason most London, New York and other big city BBQ places don't produce meat with the right level of smokiness, is because the ventilation in the professional kitchens that the law requires draws the smoke out too fast. When you smoke food you want some convection or lingering of the smoke, otherwise it just passes the meat without touching it.

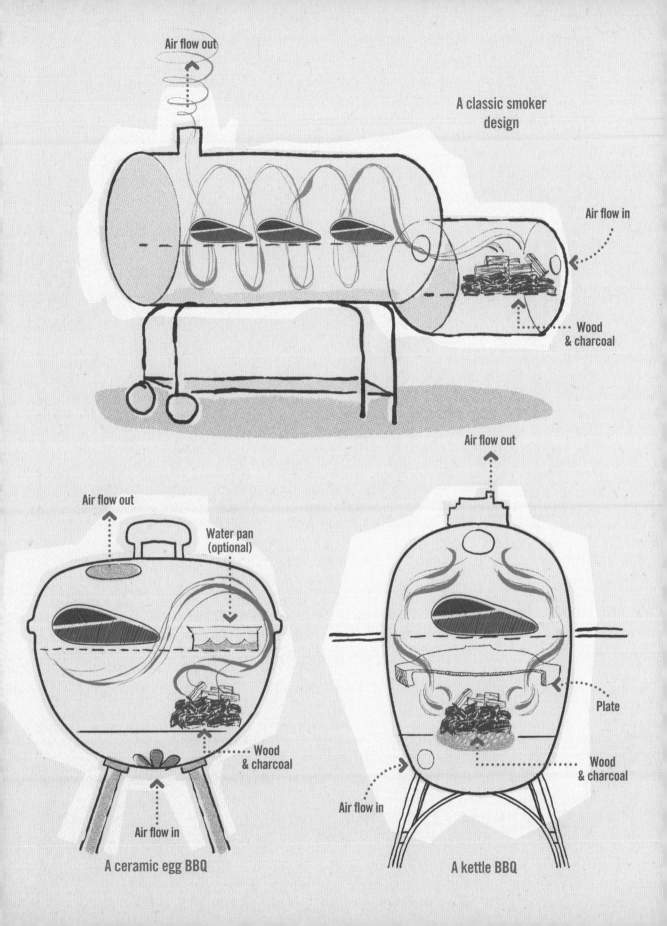

Air flow out

A classic smoker design

Air flow in

Wood & charcoal

Air flow out

Air flow out

Water pan (optional)

Plate

Wood & charcoal

Wood & charcoal

Air flow in

Air flow in

A ceramic egg BBQ

A kettle BBQ

BBQ methods

If you think I'm going to give you failsafe timings for cooking with a BBQ, you're reading the wrong book. Maybe there's a magic cookbook that will help you out somewhere, but anyone who tells you that they know a golden rule is the same guy that told you about a failsafe stock market formula. If I did have this knowledge, this book would be way more expensive to buy.

Perfect timings are pure fiction because there are too many variables. Cooking on wood and charcoal means you have to allow for wind, outside heat, type of charcoal, type of wood, type of BBQ, airflow, how clean or dirty your BBQ is, the exact position of the meat in your BBQ, and so on and on. What I can do is give you general timings and temperatures, and tell you what to look out for and what the meat feels and looks like when it's done.

Temperature is a great indicator, but always trust feel over temperature when it comes to barbecuing.

Remember that it's better to undercook than overcook – you can always cook some more in the oven, but you cannot turn back time.

The timings here are based on cooking in a ceramic-egg-style smoker or a good-quality kettle BBQ (see diagrams on page 188).

If you have a smoker that is less heat-efficient (cheaper or more rustic and home-made) the fluctuations in temperature can mean longer cook times.

Beef short ribs

1.5-2KG, SERVES 4-6

Short ribs are four bones that lie along the chuck. You need 1.5–2kg short ribs for 4–6 people. There only are two racks of short ribs on each animal, and due to their popularity it's not inconceivable that a butcher will pass off the beef belly ribs in place of short ribs. These will still taste great but will have a greater concentration of solid fat – and the butcher should tell you what he's selling you.

When buying short ribs, look for one muscle of meat above the bones. Quite often there is also a layer of chuck meat on the bone to make the rack look bigger, which means there are two muscle groups, easily identifiable as there will be a line of fat or sinew separating them. Trouble is that the chuck meat doesn't cook in the same way as it is leaner, so it will be dry and overcooked when the rib meat is perfect.

Short ribs that have good marbling can take lots of heat and rarely dry out, so make sure it's good meat from a well-reared animal. Even if the ribs are thin, you can successfully cook them.

SMOKER COOKING TEMPERATURE:
130–140°C
COOKING TIME: 5–7 hours
END INTERNAL MEAT TEMPERATURE:
92–94°C

There is very little to prep in a short rib. Some people like to take the layer of skin off the bone side but I don't bother. I just take the ribs out of the fridge, add a rub and get them straight on the BBQ, bone side down.

Let the size of the rib guide you to how long it's going to take to cook. A thin rib with no more than 3cm of meat will likely cook in 5 hours, whilst a rib cut 5cm or thicker will take at least 7 hours. Big grain-fed American USDA short ribs might take up to 9 or 10 hours.

After 4 hours, check the ribs and repeat every 30 minutes after that. What you're looking for is for the meat to have some give. Take it between your thumb and forefinger and give it a squeeze: it should feel loose and bouncy. Another test is to pierce a skewer through the meat all down the length of the bone. If the skewer goes through without resistance, the ribs are done. To make sure they're really okay, you need a probe thermometer.

Beef is easier to get right than pork, as you have to go a long way to overcook it. Usually people do the opposite. Short ribs can probably be left in the smoker for another hour after they're near done, and unless they're way too thin they should still be okay.

When the ribs are done, let the meat cool to 60°C (about 30 minutes) before slicing it off the bone – cut at right angles to the bone and then into slices in the direction of the bone. Or just bite into the meat on the bone like a caveman.

Ox cheek

800G-1KG, SERVES 1-2

Ox cheek is maybe my favourite cut to BBQ. It smokes brilliantly and becomes soft and sticky. Cheeks are offal, which means they're cut off the animal in slaughter, but they are gaining popularity, so most butchers should be able to supply them. To serve 1–2 people, you need 800g–1kg ox cheek.

SMOKER COOKING TEMPERATURE:
130–140°C
COOKING TIME: 4–6 hours
END INTERNAL MEAT TEMPERATURE:
92–94°C

Get your butcher to trim any sinew off the cheek. Other than this, there is little prep to do. Just add a rub and go.

Ox cheeks can overcook more easily than beef short ribs. You can test for give in the same way, but there is another clue to look for. The cheeks are pretty much there when you see shards of hard collagen starting to form on the underside – these look like stalactites. Cheeks have a thick layer of collagen in the centre, which needs to melt and soften before the meat becomes soft. The shards are the sign that this has started to happen, so you can be sure that the cheeks are almost ready and you need to watch them more closely. Other than that, a soft bouncy feel and a temperature thermometer are the best indicators.

Beef featherblade

2 K G , SERVES 5 - 8

This comes from the shoulder blade area of the cow. The muscle group there has a long layer of tough sinew through the middle, but there is also some great lean meat that yields flat iron/butler steaks. Taken as a whole, the featherblade is a cut that I think almost rivals brisket, and it's far easier to cook. A 2kg featherblade joint will serve 5–8 people.

SMOKER COOKING TEMPERATURE: 120–130°C
COOKING TIME: 6–8 hours
END INTERNAL MEAT TEMPERATURE: 85–90°C

Trim off any excess fat and outside sinew, and add your rub. Put the meat in the smoker and cook it, without moving it, for at least 4 hours. After that, keep checking it every 30 minutes. Unlike brisket, you're not looking for that squishy softness. When the internal temperature is around 88°C, it should be starting to give; if you stick in a thin skewer there should be no resistance through the centre – when the internal sinew has started to collapse, the meat is done.

Let it cool to 60°C, then slice. Or cool completely and chill, then slice off burger-sized pieces and pan-fry to order.

Beef brisket

5 - 6 KG, SERVES 8 - 12

I'm not going to tell you that you can cook your brisket at home like the great Texas BBQ chefs without putting in the same amount of effort as those guys do. But if you really want to and fancy the challenge, here are the steps to take. Be warned, though: this shit ain't easy. Also, to cook brisket exactly like the stuff you had in Texas, you need American prime USDA meat or something similar. I'm not a great fan of importing beef, from a sustainability level, but good brisket is all about corn-feeding and bulk. Whilst the results when we barbecue most cuts of beef in this country are as good as their American counterparts, beef for brisket needs to be corn-finished at least. You can get good brisket here but it's difficult, and without intensive corn-feeding, the variables of the finish in cattle are much higher.

SMOKER COOKING TEMPERATURE:
120–130°C
COOKING TIME: 12–14 hours
END INTERNAL MEAT TEMPERATURE:
89–94°C

Cooking brisket is hard – if you want meat that doesn't make you cry or make you want to quit your job as a chef and get a job in a bar, then this method is not for you.

STEP 1: Buy a brisket that is at least 4cm thick at the smallest point of the 'flat' (see 8-hour Super-wrapped Brisket on page 200). A 5–6kg brisket will feed 8–12 people. You really need to buy an American prime USDA brisket for this, which you can get from an online supplier.

STEP 2: Trim your brisket so you have a 1–2cm layer of fat coverage, then cover it in your favourite rub.

STEP 3: Prepare the smoker. Add a water pan to keep a gentle flow of humidity in the air inside. Place the brisket from fridge-cold, fat side up, in the smoker and leave it there untouched for 5 hours minimum, topping up the wood and maintaining the fire if necessary to keep the heat constant.

STEP 4: Check it every 30 minutes from there on. When the meat reaches 73°C internally, take it out of the smoker (if you don't have a probe thermometer, take it out after around 5–6 hours). Wrap it in peach paper/butcher's paper or foil.

STEP 5: Put it back in the smoker, or into your oven at 120°C, and cook for a further 6 hours, then every 30 minutes thereafter give it a feel or temperature check. When done, the brisket should feel like a relaxed bum cheek all over (crude but accurate).

STEP 6: Take it out and let it cool for 1–2 hours until it cools to roughly 60°C. If you wrapped it in foil, unwrap and give it a quick blast back in the smoker, or in a 180°C oven, to firm up the crust (if you wrapped it in peach paper/butcher's paper this shouldn't be necessary).

STEP 7: Slice and eat immediately. Once you've sliced a hot brisket it doesn't have a huge life span.

8-hour super-wrapped brisket

5-6KG, SERVES 8-12

There really is nothing to touch a properly cooked brisket, whether USDA or European grass-fed. The flavour hit of a well-fed cow's boob is something akin to meat heaven. If you want some of that flavour without having to stay up all night stoking a fire using the method on page 198, then try this home cheat method. It won't make you the next Aaron Franklin or Wayne Mueller, but it might produce BBQ brisket better than most of the stuff you taste in the UK.

Use this method for grass-fed brisket only. The idea behind this process is to completely eliminate the stall (see page 186). This isn't necessary with prime USDA high-fat beef, but because European beef has less fat marbling in the 'flat' we can't afford any stall.

By eliminating the stall we're speeding up the cook, and despite the moisture-loss issue the stall does benefit by increasing the time spent cooking out the collagen in the 'point' specifically, which we don't have here. That's why even though you hit core temperature, the meat won't be quite tender. It should be really close though, and all you'll then need is a really low-temperature cook to finish it off. You definitely don't need 6 hours more cooking time.

To understand this recipe you need to understand the two muscle groups in the brisket. The 'point', which is the fatty breast muscle or 'cow boob', has a good level of fat and collagen. If you were to buy this by itself, the process would be much like cooking any other slow-cooked beef. The other muscle, the 'flat', which sits underneath and extends beyond the point, is much leaner, even in prime USDA meat.

The art of a good brisket BBQ is to balance out the cooking of the two through prolonged low-temperature cooking. In practice, though, this isn't necessary as they are really easy to separate during cooking and finish separately.

SMOKER COOKING TEMPERATURE: 120°C
COOKING TIME: 8 hours
END INTERNAL MEAT TEMPERATURE: It's all about feel.

STEP 1: TRIM

Buy a 5–6kg grass-fed brisket as it comes off the carcass, which will serve 8–12 people. Don't trim it at all; with USDA you want to trim, with grass-fed cook with what you have as it's all meat. Trimming it too lean, like you might with prime USDA meat, will put you on the back foot. Instead, take off any huge lumps of fat. Also take off any large patches of sinew and, if it's been dry-aged, wet with water until any bits that are too dry have moistened up.

STEP 2: SMOKE

Wet the fridge-cold brisket with your hands, rubbing the water in until it is moist. Cover it with your favourite rub, then throw it into the smoker at 120°C with a good amount of wood. Put in a small water pan, then cook for 5 hours. Take it out no matter what the internal temperature is (it will never be higher than 73°C if the meat is unwrapped, because of the stall). Once it's out, wrap it first in foil, then tightly in lots of clingfilm (four or five layers) and then in foil again. The clingfilm will not melt at this temperature but we are using foil to stop the contact with the meat in any case. If you're worried, just use foil and keep it tight. The reason we don't use peach/butcher's paper here is because we want to stop the brisket 'breathing'.

STEP 3: THE SUPERWRAP COOK

Put the wrapped brisket back into your smoker at 120°C. The internal temperature should rise by around 10°C every hour, so after 2 hours check the 'flat'. If it's beginning to soften and/or has reached 85°C, then pull the brisket out. If not, give the brisket another hour or so, checking after 30 minutes.

Meanwhile, set your oven to 75°C and place a roasting tray inside. When the 'flat' hits temperature, take the brisket out of the smoker. The fattier 'point' muscle will still be well undercooked and tough, so you need to slice this off (see diagram below) to separate the muscles. There is a fat layer between the two and it is possible to separate them merely by pulling them apart with your hands.

If you struggle with this, just slice it in two down the middle so that you have one side that is just flat and one side with the point and some flat beneath it.

Wrap up the flat separately in foil and place in the low oven to finish cooking.

Rewrap the fattier point in foil, then put it back in the smoker at 120°C and continue to cook for at least another hour. If you're in a rush, you can ramp up the smoker temperature a little but no higher than 140°C.

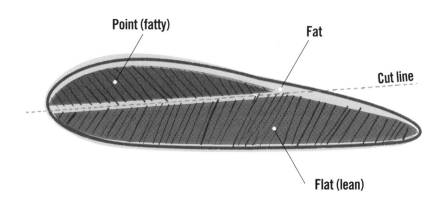

Point (fatty) — Fat — Cut line — Flat (lean)

8-hour super-wrapped continued

Once the point is starting to get soft, take it out and place it in the oven with the flat.

Continue cooking until both muscles are soft (feeling like a relaxed bum cheek). Internal temperature from now on doesn't matter – it's all about feel. And at that temp it will be hard to overcook either.

STEP 4: SERVE OR CHILL

Leave the brisket to cool to 60°C – this takes about an hour – then slice and serve. If you don't want to eat the brisket right away, you can keep it wrapped in the fridge whole. To reheat the next day, simply chuck it, unwrapped, into a 150°C oven – about an hour for the point and 45 minutes for the flat.

Alternatively, cut the brisket into slices or cubes from cold and reheat with a little vegetable oil in a frying pan like a steak. It can last up to 4 days this way. Brisket steaks with some fried eggs make an extremely memorable breakfast. It's a great meat for lots of other dishes too.

Lamb ribs

SERVES 3 - 6

Known to British butchers as bone-in lamb breast, this is basically the whole belly cut of lamb with the bones attached. In beef it would be the brisket plus the plate; in pork it's the whole belly. Lamb belly is smaller than pork belly, but it does have the advantage of a huge fat and collagen content, which makes it far easier to cook than pork ribs. I've overcooked lamb ribs a million times and they're still good to eat. A whole slab of ribs will feed 3–6 people.

SMOKER COOKING TEMPERATURE:
130–140°C
COOKING TIME: 5–7 hours
END INTERNAL MEAT TEMPERATURE:
90–96°C

This is a straight hot cook. Apply your favourite rub to the ribs and set your smoker to 130°C. Place the slab, meat side up, in the smoker.

After cooking, cool the ribs down to 60°C, then slice into individual ribs and serve.

These also taste great if they're chilled, then sliced and chargrilled. You can blacken lamb a bit more than any other meat to get that Lebanese vibe. Serve them with mint sauce or with something fresh and creamy like tzatziki.

Pork spare ribs

SERVES 5-9

When following an American BBQ method, the advantage of cooking pork rather than beef cuts is that in general our pigs, unlike cows, are more similar to their counterparts in the US – in their feed and the way they're raised to be high in fat, and in being roughly similar in size. We also have a long history of native breeds with stunning flavour profiles. A drawback, though, is that butchery methods are very different, and the cuts used in the US seem alien to many of our butchers.

However, this is mostly irrelevant because it's only a matter of description and explaining what you want. If you just ask for pork spare ribs in the UK, you'll get pork spare ribs but only the skinniest of skinny spare ribs. This is because the spare rib comes from the underside of the belly and the belly is highly profitable for butchers. They remove the rib bones, leaving as much of the belly meat off as possible. What we really want is to have some of that meat left on the bones.

A belly as a whole cut has a large rectangular rib bone section surrounded by bone-free areas. Pork belly ribs are basically this whole rib section. Pork spare ribs are this section with a little trimmed off the top, just under the skin; St Louis are spare ribs with the back rib section (or rib tips) trimmed off to make an even smaller cut. So instead of asking for spare ribs, tell your butcher you want the whole rib section of the belly. Ask him to remove the skin and to trim the first layer of fat on the belly, leaving a meaty rib section with a little fat. You could ask him to trim it further to be more traditional, but for me the whole thick belly is good. I like a meaty rib.

Next, get him to cut out the ten largest bones in a rectangle going across just behind where the red meat starts behind the white rib section. If you want, you can ask him to go closer into the ribs across the round protruding joints – this is the famous St Louis cut – but to me it seems a little wasteful. Have the butcher remove the layer of sinew on the back of the ribs, or you can do this yourself pretty easily by prising up a section with a blunt knife and pulling it off with a dry cloth held in your fingers.

You don't need to waste anything – ask the butcher to mince the leftover meat for you, to use in another dish. And keep the skin to make crackling, if you like. You'll end up paying more per kilo but you'll get what you want. The resulting slab of spare ribs will serve 5–9 people.

SMOKER COOKING TEMPERATURE: 120–130°C
COOKING TIME: 4–5 hours
END INTERNAL MEAT TEMPERATURE: 88–92°C

Pork spare ribs continued

Rub your ribs up, then place the slab, meat side up, in the smoker. Have a little water pan in there too. Leave untouched for at least 2 hours before you start checking for colour – this is the best indicator of when ribs have had enough smoke. Pork will turn a brownish to red shade when it has been smoked enough. The colour will vary by the breed and age of the pig, but generally it will change dramatically to this colour range. Also, the smoke should still smell good. You can wrap it at this stage in peach/butcher's paper but, if it is fatty enough, I don't really bother.

Put the wrapped pork back in the smoker and give it roughly another 2 hours. After an hour, start checking it regularly (every 20 minutes) for doneness. For me, the tell is a feeling of tenderness between the thickest two ribs when pressed between my fingers. Some people hold up the slab of spare ribs to see how far it bends (it should bend easily but not break), or stick a skewer between the rib bones – if it goes through without resistance, the pork is done. The desired temperature is about 90°C.

When you're happy, leave the slab of ribs wrapped at room temperature until cooled to about 60°C (about 30 minutes), then slice between the bones and serve. If you want the ribs saucy, you can paint some BBQ sauce (see recipes, pages 224–228) on once they've cooled, then place them back on a grill in a hot smoker, or under the grill in your oven, for a few minutes.

If you've cooked these perfectly, they shouldn't 'fall off the bone' but rather be just tender enough so you can see your teeth marks when you bite into them.

Pork ribs

Lamb ribs

Pork shoulder

4-5KG, SERVES 6-10

Pulled pork is so popular these days that almost every pub in the country has it on their menu. Despite its popularity, though, it's one of the most misunderstood and badly executed dishes I've ever seen. True pulled pork isn't ripped apart with a fork or pulled apart until it's just textureless strands of unidentifiable meat wrapped in a sauce to add back all the lost moisture. In fact, you don't 'pull' pork – it should almost fall apart itself and remain in chunks, which although incredibly tender, still hold on to their own moisture without the aid of a sauce. Pulled really is the wrong word to use. I prefer to say 'broken' pork as what you really want are chunks, not strands or shreds.

For good pulled pork you need to start with a boneless pork neck end joint or butt. A 4–5kg joint will serve 6–10 people. Ask the butcher to remove the skin but keep on a good layer of fat. You want at least a 1–2cm layer of fat but preferably thicker on top.

> **SMOKER COOKING TEMPERATURE:** 120°C
> **COOKING TIME:** 12–14 hours (plus reheating)
> **END INTERNAL MEAT TEMPERATURE:** 92–95°C

STEP 1: SMOKE
Rub it up, then smoke at 120°C for 6 hours without opening your smoker.

STEP 2: COOK
Wrap the butt tightly in foil or peach/butcher's paper and put it back in the smoker. Leave to cook for 6–8 hours or until the pork reaches an internal temperature of 92–95°C. (If you don't have a great smoker for such long cooks, this stage could be done in the oven at 120°C.)

STEP 3: CHILL
Whilst still wrapped up, press down on the parcel to start breaking up the pork inside and make a flatter easier-to-chill shape. Leave the pork to cool for a while at room temperature. You can eat it now but to make it even better, chill in the fridge for at least 24 hours. Pork changes dramatically when it is cooled and reheated. Much like last night's leftover curry that tasted better the next day, it's all about the meat reabsorbing its own juices and tenderising further.

STEP 4: PULL AND REHEAT
Unwrap the cold meat and grab chunks off with your fingers. Either warm through in the oven at 150°C for 30 minutes or, even better, in a dry (there will be plenty of fat) hot frying pan, adding more rub and a little BBQ sauce (see recipes, pages 224–228) if this takes your fancy. It's great to get a bit of colour and crispness to offset the softness of the meat and add extra flavour and texture.

Whole chicken

1.6-2KG BIRD, SERVES 2-4

To do this, you follow exactly the same method as given for the roast Slutty chicken (see page 96), except instead of a slow-cook in the oven we are doing a slow-cook in the smoker. A 1.6–2kg bird will feed 2–4 people.

SMOKER COOKING TEMPERATURE: 120–130°C
COOKING TIME: 1–1½ hours
END INTERNAL BREAST TEMPERATURE: 68–70°C (leg temp will naturally be higher)

Give your chicken your favourite rub and set your smoker to 120°C.

As the smoker temperature will not be as accurate as the oven, you need to be more flexible with the cooking time than with a roast chicken. Use a probe thermometer to check that the breasts hit 68°C; with touch, this is the point where the breasts just begin to firm up. Don't cook the chicken longer than this to be safe because it will self-cook a little further once it's out of the smoker, and you can always give it more time after it's jointed. That way you avoid cooking the whole thing dry.

You can either eat the chicken straight away, or leave it to cool at room temperature for an hour, then roast in the oven at 240°C for 15 minutes to get a crispier skin. Try served with Gochujang mayo (page 232).

Chicken wings

Rub the wings with your favourite rub and place in the 120°C smoker to cook for about an hour. During the last 10 minutes in the smoker, you might want to give these a little sauce baste (try Green chilli and soy chicken glaze, page 231).

Or deep-fry and then plunge them into a BBQ sauce.

For me, the stickier the better – wings are a bit of messy fun. When you start getting serious over chicken wings, you should start re-evaluating your priorities in life.

SMOKER COOKING TEMPERATURE: 120–130°C
COOKING TIME: 1 hour
END INTERNAL MEAT TEMPERATURE: 68–72°C

You can either eat these straight away, or chill completely and then deep-fry until crispy.

RUBS, SAUCES AND SIDES FOR BBQS

A note on meat rubs

The word 'rub' is a little confusing. Basically rubbing is just seasoning, shaking it on to your meat and leaving it there, as you would with any kind of seasoning. There is no need to complicate the ingredients you use. You can season just with salt, if you wish. That said, what I like to do with all meat to be smoked is to wet the surface with a little water and make a paste with some of the rub, then sprinkle the rest of the rub over the meat like rain. I finish with some extra cracked black pepper for spice and to create a rougher texture, which draws in more smoke.

For me, the more rough-textured the rub is, the better the flavour. The way smoke moves around your meat in the smoker means most of the smoke doesn't land on the surface. What you want the rub to do, along with any other rough surface on the meat, is help to displace the smoke stream so it creates extra chances of it hitting the meat. Also, I like the crust that comes from a rough rub.

The lesson to be learned here is that there is no mystery to BBQ rubs. Don't be fooled into thinking there is a secret ingredient in any of them unless it's MSG, which does help make things moreish. Your focus should be on the smoke – that's the flavour that should stand out.

Don't worry about how long a rub should be on the meat. I tend to do it at the last minute but the night before is fine too.

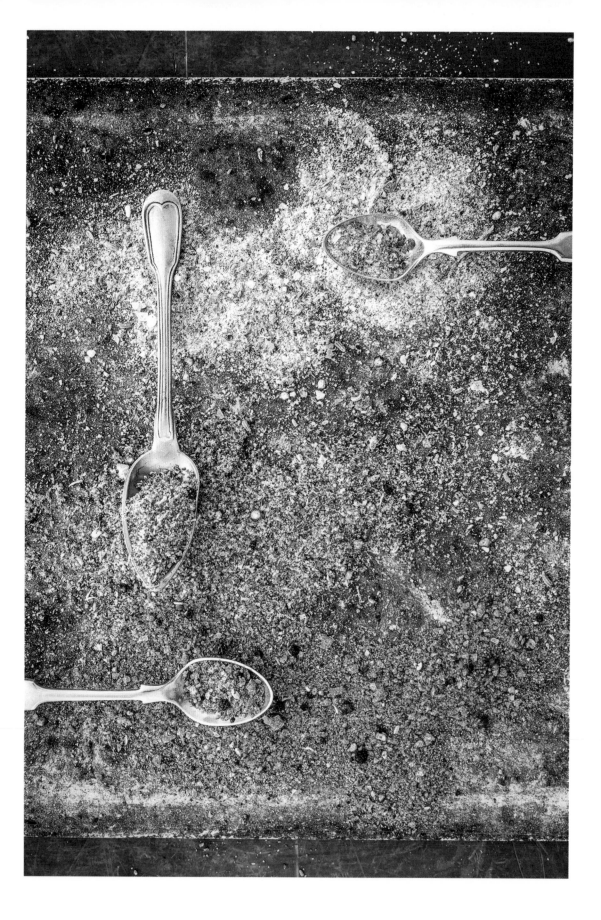

Salt and pepper rub

It might seem a little silly to post this as a recipe but it's what goes on most of the barbecued meats I cook at home. I think smoked meat should taste of smoke and meat. Whilst other rubs are lots of fun, if the meat is good and the smoke is good, this is all you need to do to season. Some people add a little garlic powder to this or sugar. It's up to you.

Maldon salt, pulsed in a blender until even but still rough (or if you can buy American kosher salt, use it as it is)
Coarsely cracked black pepper

Mixing these together can be a pain as the pepper separates and you can get an uneven distribution. Unless I'm doing lots of briskets, I usually keep the salt and pepper separate and just season as I would any roast or steak.

Wet your meat with a little water, then cover it in salt first. Go heavy for cuts like brisket and pork shoulder, as the volume requires more seasoning. Go lighter on smaller cuts, such as short rib or ox cheek. Then go over it with pepper. The biggest difference between American BBQ places is pepper quantity – in Austin, Texas, for example, they go heavy on pepper. I like it but it's all down to personal taste.

Top to bottom: Salt cure for pork,
Thai rub, Everyday rub

Everyday rub

This is a more classic rub, mainly for pork and chicken although it can be used for any meat. The amount of sugar is a little controversial but the purpose is not really crust-development so much as balance. You can pretty much blanket-cover with this stuff and you won't over-season because of the level of sugar to salt. Also it's delicious. You can use it on any vegetable side or your mac and cheese. It goes into my chicken-fried steak batter, and I've even served it on ice cream. The basic sugar to salt ratio is what's fundamental – the rest of the ingredients are just flavour accents, so feel free to play around with the spices and herbs. If you do want to reduce the sugar, be careful not to overdo it. These quantities make lots but it will keep for months if not years.

125g Maldon salt, pulsed in
    a blender until looser
    but still a little rough
100g coarsely cracked
    black pepper
25g garlic salt
150g dark soft brown sugar
150g caster sugar
75g paprika

FOR THE SPICES
5g cumin seeds
5g caraway seeds
10g fennel seeds
5g coriander seeds
2 bay leaves

Toast the spices in a dry pan, then blitz in a spice grinder or with a pestle and mortar until roughly ground. Mix with all the other ingredients and store in a tightly covered container. You can keep this in a cool, dark place pretty much as long as you like.

Thai rub

This is a bit of fun, great on pork or chicken. Mix it with tempura flour for salt and pepper squid too. If you can't find dried shrimp powder, buy dried shrimp, freeze and pulse in a blender. I'm not suggesting that you should add MSG to this, but it tastes pretty stunning if you do. Up to you though… no pressure.

125g Maldon salt, pulsed in a blender until even but still rough
100g coarsely cracked black pepper
150g dark soft brown sugar
150g caster sugar
75g gochugaru (Korean chilli powder)
25g dried shrimp powder
15g garlic powder
15g ground ginger

FOR THE SPICES
10g coriander seeds
5g cumin seeds
2 dried lime leaves

Toast the spices in a dry pan, then blitz in a spice grinder or with a pestle and mortar until roughly ground. Mix with all the other ingredients and store in a tightly covered container. You can keep this in a cool, dark place pretty much as long as you like.

Salt cure for pork

Before slow-smoking a whole belly I like to cure it first for a day or two using this mix. Sometimes I play around with shoulders too or pig's heads, or mix the cure with some chopped parsley and a little finely chopped fresh red chilli to use as a filling in a rolled joint. You can also use this to cure most white fish. If you're not washing off the salt cure mix before cooking, add it less liberally.

20g fennel seeds
5g garlic salt
3 bay leaves
5g coarsely cracked
   black pepper
5 juniper berries
75g Maldon salt
Grated lemon, lime or
   orange zest

Toast the fennel seeds, garlic salt, bay, pepper and juniper berries in a dry pan, then blitz in a spice grinder or in a pestle and mortar to a coarse mix. Add the salt and pulse to blend.

After the salt cure, add a little lemon, lime or orange zest to the meat, or a bit of each.

Jerk rub

This is less of a rub and more of a sauce. You can rub it over the meat before cooking, but I tend to add it afterwards as the flavour is fresher and sharper. This can also be turned into a great sauce by mixing it with mayonnaise, soured cream or a BBQ sauce (see page 224).

1 tablespoon allspice
   berries
1 tablespoon coarsely
   cracked black
   peppercorns
½ teaspoon ground
   cinnamon
½ teaspoon grated nutmeg
1 tablespoon thyme
   leaves, chopped
1 fresh Scotch Bonnet
   chilli, finely chopped
1 tablespoon dark soft
   brown sugar
1 teaspoon Maldon salt
2 tablespoons dark soy
   sauce
4 spring onions, finely
   chopped (use the white
   part and most of the
   green)
Juice of 1 lime

Put all of the ingredients, apart from the spring onions and lime juice, in a blender or food processor and pulse together, then stir through the spring onions and lime juice at the last minute. If you want a wetter mixture, just add cold water until you get a nice consistency.

Vinegar sauce

Jerk rub

Sauces

All these sauces can be used as a glaze for finishing meats in the smoker or once they're out, or served as a dip alongside. I don't have any preference for which sauces go with which meats. They're all good and will go just as nicely with a bowl of chips.

Blackened romesco sauce

Bacon and bourbon red wine syrup

Pear and miso chutney

House BBQ sauce

MAKES ABOUT 400ML

I've made sauces with hundreds of ingredients and I have to say, after years of trying this and that, simple is always better. This is my basic sweet and a little spicy BBQ sauce. For a less spicy sauce, you can replace half of the hot sauce with cider vinegar. If you don't have a smoker, don't worry – the sauce will still taste good.

240ml tomato ketchup
80ml Frank's Red Hot
   Original Pepper Sauce
80ml Worcestershire sauce
80ml cold water
30g unsalted butter, cubed
2 garlic cloves, thickly
   sliced
Cracked black pepper

Mix together the ketchup, pepper and Worcestershire sauces, and water in a heatproof container. Stick it in the smoker at 120°C and leave for at least an hour, adding more water if the sauce dries up too much. If you're cooking meat in the smoker and it has levels, smoking the sauce under that meat won't do any harm. Once the sauce is out, add more water until you have the required thickness.

If you aren't smoking the sauce, simply leave out the water.

Melt a little of the butter in a saucepan and roast the garlic until brown. Add the sauce and cook for a few minutes, then turn down the heat and add the rest of the butter, cube by cube, stirring well after each addition until emulsified.

Strain the sauce and finish with cracked pepper, as much as you like. It shouldn't need any salt. This will keep for weeks in a sterilised bottle or jar in the fridge.

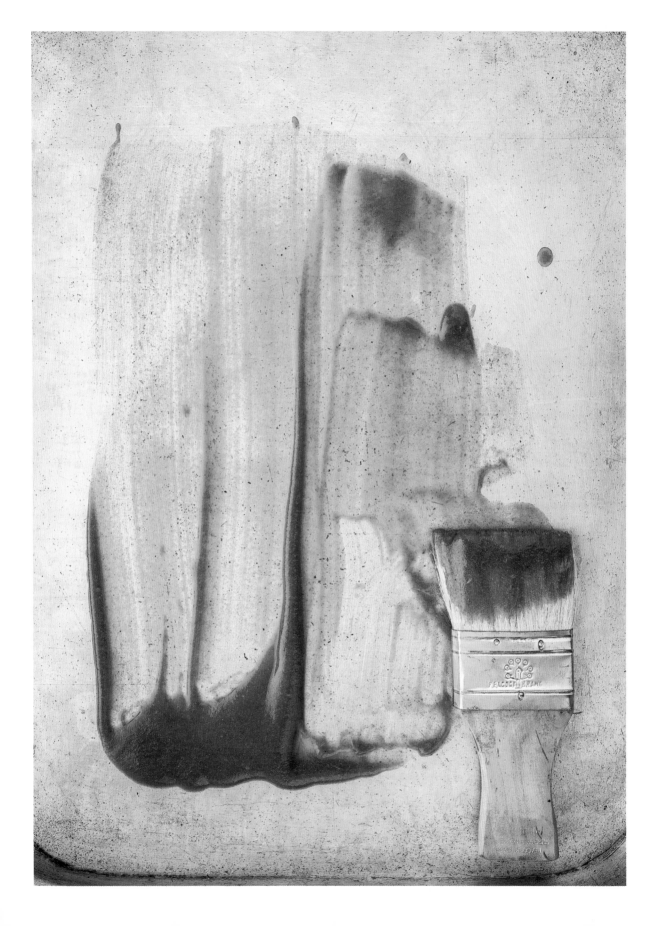

Mezcal BBQ sauce

MAKES ABOUT 400ML

This is a spicy one. No need to smoke it, but if you want to add some juices from the meat, go ahead. It won't hurt.

240ml tomato ketchup
80ml Frank's Red Hot Original Pepper Sauce
80ml cider vinegar
80ml Worcestershire sauce
30ml mezcal (Mexican spirit similar to tequila)
30ml water
20g tinned chipotle chillies in adobo sauce/paste, blended to a purée
30g unsalted butter, cubed
2 garlic cloves, thickly sliced
Chopped coriander
Juice of 1 lime

Mix together the ketchup, pepper sauce, vinegar, Worcestershire sauce, mezcal, water and chilli purée.

Melt a little of the butter in a saucepan and roast the garlic until brown, then add the ketchup mixture. Bring to the boil and reduce by a third. Turn down the heat and add the rest of the butter, cube by cube, stirring in each addition until emulsified.

Strain the sauce and finish with some chopped coriander and lime juice to taste. Serve warm.

Korean BBQ sauce

Vinegar smoker baste/mop

Green chilli and soy
chicken glaze

Mezcal BBQ sauce

Korean BBQ sauce

MAKES 300ML

My staple sauce. I use this more than anything else – in my pulled or 'broken' pork, on my beef short ribs and also as a marinade for beef tartare.

100ml sriracha (hot chilli
    sauce)
100ml soy sauce
100ml toasted sesame oil
4 garlic cloves, peeled

Blitz together all the ingredients in a blender. That's all folks.

If you want more of a sweet glaze, warm the sauce and add soft brown sugar to taste. If you want to use it as a chicken wing sauce, mix in 150g unsalted butter, cube by cube, and serve warm.

Vinegar sauce

MAKES 270ML

Meat, meet vinegar. This is not a Carolina-style sauce but it has the same ideals. The mix of sriracha, hoisin and soy without the vinegar will make a pretty good sweet sauce all by itself. You can add the vinegar until you're happy with the flavour, but I like this ratio best. Dip in your fresh BBQ, straight off the grill.

3 tablespoons sriracha (hot chilli sauce)

3 tablespoons hoisin sauce

3 tablespoons dark soy sauce

9 tablespoons pickling liquor from a jar of gherkins (or cider, rice or white wine vinegar)

Mix all the ingredients together and keep in a sealed, sterilised jar in the fridge for 3–4 days before using.

If you want a little body, before using you can gently heat the sauce and mix in some unsalted butter, but don't store it with the butter added.

Vinegar smoker baste/mop

MAKES ABOUT 500ML

You can use the Vinegar Sauce on page 229 for basting, but I like a mop that is a little less vinegary. I also like the effect of more soy – even once reduced it doesn't ever overpower the meat. We're only using this to essentially wet the meat to attract more smoke, and for me it's only big cuts of meat that need long, slow cooking and more smoke. Smaller cuts I just straight cook with no mop.

250ml white wine vinegar
300ml water
100g caster sugar
40ml soy sauce

Mix all the ingredients together, stirring until the sugar has dissolved.

Green chilli and soy chicken glaze

MAKES ENOUGH FOR 2 WHOLE CHICKENS

Sticky, spicy, sweet and sour, this is my perfect wing sauce or a glaze for whole chickens. For the spice-averse, try it with all Frank's and no Tabasco, and drop the green chilli.

100g apricot jam
20ml soy sauce
10ml white wine vinegar
5ml Tabasco sauce
5ml Frank's Red Hot
    Original Pepper Sauce
1 fresh green chilli, sliced
Lime juice

Put everything, except the lime juice, in a saucepan and bring to the boil, stirring occasionally. Leave to cool.

Dunk your barbecued wings into the sauce, then drench in freshly squeezed lime juice.

Buffalo wing sauce

MAKES ENOUGH FOR 10-15 WINGS

Classic and easy. If you want it a bit more spicy, use Frank's Xtra Hot Sauce or replace 50ml of the hot sauce with Tabasco.

100ml Frank's Red Hot
   Original Pepper Sauce
100g unsalted butter, cubed

Warm the hot sauce in a small saucepan and then slowly stir in the butter, cube by cube, stirring well after each addition until emulsified. Serve warm and immediately.

Gochujang mayo

MAKES ABOUT 500ML

Creamy and slightly spicy, and with a huge umami kick, this goes great with beef and lamb. There is nothing wrong with using shop-bought mayo and just mixing in the chilli paste. This saves a lot of time and tastes pretty much the same. But this is a cookbook, so...

4 free-range egg yolks
About 30g gochujang
   (Korean hot chilli paste)
500ml vegetable oil
1 tablespoon white wine
   vinegar
Juice of ½ lemon
Maldon salt and pepper

You can make the mayonnaise in a blender or using a whisk. Blitz or whisk up your yolks with the 30g chilli paste and a little salt, then begin adding the oil in a slow, steady stream, blitzing/whisking until the mix starts to thicken. If it gets too thick, add a little room-temperature water. Once you have a good consistency, add the vinegar and lemon juice to taste. Season with salt and pepper.

Add more chilli paste to taste to make a dark orange sauce with a little kick.

Gochujang mayo

Sriracha salad cream

Smoked and roasted
chicken aioli

Buffalo wing sauce

Smoked and roasted chicken aioli

MAKES ABOUT 500ML

What's the best thing to serve with chicken? If your answer is 'chicken', you get a gold star. I love to eat this with fresh grilled asparagus and a mountain of BBQ'd chicken. Here's how to do it.

4 free-range egg yolks
2 teaspoons Dijon mustard
1 tablespoon white wine
   vinegar
2 garlic cloves, crushed
Juice of ½ lemon
Maldon salt and pepper

FOR THE CHICKEN OIL
300g chicken wings
500ml vegetable oil

Make the chicken oil. First place your wings in a smoker at 120°C and leave for at least 2 hours.

Set your oven to 160°C. Remove the wings from the smoker, place in a roasting tray and roast for 30 minutes. Cool, then chill.

Add the wings to your oil in a saucepan and cook on a medium heat until you can start to smell the aroma from the oil. Remove from the heat, cover and leave to cool. The longer you leave it, the better the flavour. I would recommend at least 24 hours in the fridge but you can give it just a few hours if you're in a rush. Strain through a fine sieve before using.

To make the mayonnaise you can use a blender or a whisk. Blitz/whisk your yolks with the mustard and a little salt, then begin adding your chicken oil in a slow, steady stream. If the mixture gets too thick, add a little room-temperature water. Once you have a good consistency, add the vinegar, garlic and lemon juice to taste. Season with salt and pepper – don't be shy to go heavy on the pepper.

This is even more delicious topped with a little crumbled crispy chicken skin (see Chicken Noodle Soup, page 171).

Bacon and bourbon red wine syrup

MAKES ABOUT 250ML

I like to dip barbecued rib tips into this and also use it to glaze chicken wings. It's also especially nice with foie gras.

200g smoked streaky bacon
    rashers
300ml bourbon whiskey
700ml red wine
100g caster sugar

In a saucepan (not non-stick), fry the bacon in batches until brown. You want to get as much bacon browning bits stuck to the bottom of the pan as possible, so keep going with each batch until there is lots of browning. If it becomes too much, add a little water to deglaze. Set the bacon aside in a freezerproof container.

Deglaze the pan with the bourbon and cook, stirring, for a few minutes. Pour into the container with the bacon. Cool, then freeze for 5 hours. The alcohol won't freeze but what you will end up with is bacon-flavoured bourbon. (You could stop here and have a drink or make a cocktail or two, and that could be that, but please persist.) Strain the bourbon.

Put the bacon bourbon, red wine and sugar in a pan and reduce until you have a thick syrup. If it gets too thick, you can add a little water. Serve warm or store in the fridge.

Sriracha salad cream

MAKES 250ML

First off, may I apologise for using sriracha in pretty much everything I make. It is tasty stuff though – I always have a bottle in my store cupboard – and this is a book of things I actually cook rather than pretend to. Salad cream is an underrated condiment in my opinion. Like the mayo recipe on page 232, feel free to use shop-bought salad cream. It's actually pretty nice. But here's how to make it if you want to. Serve this sauce with chargrilled vegetables straight off the BBQ. (Photo opposite.)

2 free-range eggs, beaten
1 tablespoon caster sugar
5 tablespoons rice wine
   vinegar
250ml whipping cream
Sriracha (hot chilli sauce),
   to taste

Whisk/beat the eggs, sugar and vinegar together in a heatproof bowl set over a pan of simmering water. Keep whisking until you can write a number 8 with the mixture on the surface. Remove from the heat.

Whip the cream in a separate bowl until stiff, then fold into the sauce. Add sriracha, folding it in, until you start getting a nice heat.

Blood orange ponzu

MAKES ABOUT 300ML

I sometimes baste meat skewers with this as they're finishing on the grill. It's also great as a dip for barbecued chicken or pork.

75ml freshly squeezed
   lime juice
25ml freshly squeezed
   blood orange juice
200ml soy sauce
½ tablespoon kombu
   powder

Mix the ingredients together in a pan and heat gently, stirring to dissolve the kombu. Serve warm.

Pear and miso chutney

MAKES ABOUT 500ML

250g caster sugar

250ml cold water

6 cloves

1 cinnamon stick

3 star anise

500g pears, peeled, cored
and diced

1 red onion, finely diced

1 red pepper, deseeded and
finely diced

15g fresh ginger, peeled
and sliced

250ml white wine vinegar

White or Korean miso

Put the sugar, water and spices in a saucepan and bring to the boil, stirring to dissolve the sugar. Once boiling, add the pears, onion, red pepper, ginger and vinegar. Cook down until syrupy, stirring occasionally.

Check the quantity and combine with an equal amount of miso. Transfer to a sterilised jar(s), then cool and seal.

Blackened romesco sauce

MAKES ABOUT 500ML

This is a hell of a sauce, dark and broody. It's great in pasta and with smoked pork ribs or chicken. I would bathe in it if I could. I don't remove any of the charred skin or the seeds from the chillies and peppers. That said, if you burn them so much that the skin becomes hard, like tough charcoal, then you probably should remove it.

4–5 large red peppers, burnt on the grill (skin intact)

4 fresh red chillies, burnt on the grill (skin intact)

2 tomatoes, cut in half and grilled (skin intact)

3 tablespoons ground almonds

1 teaspoon ground cinnamon

4 tablespoons gochugaru (Korean chilli powder)

2 tablespoons smoked paprika

3 preserved lemons

6 garlic cloves, peeled

Juice of 3 small lemons

Maldon salt, to taste

Blitz everything together in a blender… simple. Use immediately.

Goat belly beans

SERVES 6-10

1 goat belly
1 litre chicken stock
1 litre water
4 x 400g tins Heinz baked
    beans
Vegetable oil, for frying
3 garlic cloves, sliced
1 onion, sliced
2 teaspoons garam
    masala
1 teaspoon ground cumin
1 teaspoon ground ancho
    chillies
200ml Madeira
300ml tomato passata
2 thyme sprigs
2 bay leaves (break the
    leaves to release more
    flavour)
50ml sherry vinegar
Maldon salt and pepper

Set the oven to 160°C. Season the belly, place it in an open casserole or roasting tray, then roast for 30 minutes until browned. Turn down the oven to 120°C, add the stock and water and leave to braise in the oven overnight or for 8 hours.

Lift the belly out of the pot. Whilst still warm, break up the meat without shredding it, discarding any bones. Drizzle over some of the braising stock to keep the meat moist. Leave to cool. Cover and keep in the fridge until needed. Keep the rest of the stock in the fridge too.

When ready to use, drain the beans of their tomato sauce.

Heat a little oil in a saucepan, add the garlic and roast until lightly browned. Add the onion and sweat until soft. Stir in the spices and cook out for 5 minutes.

Deglaze with the Madeira, then add the goat stock and bring to the boil. Simmer until reduced and thick. Stir in the passata, drained beans, herbs and picked goat meat.

Pour into a suitable container (uncovered) and place in the smoker at 120°C. Cook for 40–60 minutes, adding water if the liquid dries out too much.

Season with the sherry vinegar and salt and pepper.

Dirty ginger rice

SERVES 4-6

New Orleans meets Vietnam. Dirty rice is something that goes well with all BBQ food, but this Asian-influenced version has another level of spice and freshness that works even better.

30g fresh ginger, peeled
30g fresh green chillies
30g garlic cloves, peeled
30g light soft brown sugar
2 tablespoons soy sauce
30g coriander stalks
Grated zest of 2 limes
Juice of 1 lime
2 cups basmati rice (see
　　recipe method)
2 cups chicken stock
2 cups water
8 chicken livers
Vegetable oil, for frying
2 spring onions, sliced
2 tablespoons chopped
　　coriander leaves
3 fresh red chillies, chopped
Maldon salt

Put the ginger, green chillies, garlic, sugar, soy, stalks, zest and juice in a blender and blitz until smooth. Set aside.

For the rice, I measure by volume because for me it's easier to work out this way. If you don't have an American cup measure you can use a teacup instead. It's not the same but it's near enough. Rinse your rice and place in a saucepan with the stock, water and a pinch of salt. Put a lid on the pan and bring to the boil, then cook for about 10 minutes until the rice is light and fluffy. Leave to one side, covered.

Fry the livers in a little oil in a hot frying pan until browned on the outside but not cooked through. Take out the livers, chop roughly and add to the rice. Heat up the frying pan again and deglaze with a little water. Add the rice mix back to the pan.

Off the heat, gradually stir the ginger mix into the rice until you find it's to your taste. It's spicy, so go slow. Finish by mixing in the spring onions, chopped coriander and red chillies. Season with salt and serve immediately.

Warm Thai salad

SERVES 3 - 6

Apart from the way it's made, this is not a traditional Thai salad. It's more about the technique and the dressing than the vegetables – pretty much any vegetable can be used, so it's very versatile. You can buy some classic Thai vegetables if you like, or fruit, but I much prefer to use what's local and seasonal because I think the vegetables will taste better. This is an ethos that drives a lot of my cooking. I'm not being a hippy about it. It just makes sense to me to use the best things you can find, rather than second-rate produce for the sake of following a recipe to the letter.

For this salad, slice the vegetables really thin because they're only gently heated rather than cooked.

Play with the way you cut them to create interest – some round, some long and thin, some in ribbons. It makes the salad look shit hot. The vegetables and fruit suggested opposite are for a spring salad.

200g light soft brown sugar

200ml water

120ml fish sauce

150ml freshly squeezed
lime juice

30g garlic paste

30g ginger paste

30g fresh green chilli

6 garlic cloves, sliced
medium-thin

Vegetable oil, for frying

100g roasted peanuts

2 tablespoons chopped
coriander

2 tablespoons chopped
mint

3 fresh Thai red chillies,
finely sliced

Grated zest of 5 limes

1 tablespoon dried shrimp
powder

FOR THE SALAD

1 blood orange, segmented

1 eating/dessert apple,
cored, sliced into
matchsticks

1 fennel bulb, thinly sliced

6 heritage radishes, thinly
sliced

4 English asparagus spears,
shaved into ribbons

1 white/yellow/green
courgette, cut into
julienne

50g freshly podded peas

3 spring onions, thinly
sliced into rounds

1 red onion, thinly sliced

In a large saucepan, dissolve the sugar in the water over a low heat to make a syrup. Remove from the heat and mix with the fish sauce and lime juice. Take a small amount of the syrup and blitz with the garlic and ginger pastes and the green chilli in a blender. Stir into the rest of the syrup to make the dressing. Set aside in the pan.

Put the sliced garlic in a pan with a little oil and fry until the slices turn a light caramel brown and are crisp. Drain the garlic on kitchen paper.

Coarsely chop the peanuts – you don't want them turned into powder, just lots of random-sized chunks.

Heat the dressing gently so it is just warm to the touch. Throw in some of your salad ingredients and toss until everything is covered with dressing, being careful not to dress too much at a time as you don't want to crowd the pan. All of the ingredients should still have bite but not taste raw. As each batch of salad is dressed, lift it out into a bowl.

Mix in most of the herbs, peanuts and red chillies, the zest and crispy garlic, then transfer to a serving dish. Finish with the shrimp powder and the rest of the peanuts, red chillies and herbs. Serve immediately.

Last-minute grilled salad

SERVES 6 - 8

This is another dish where the idea is not to dictate to you what you should or shouldn't use. Instead, it's about what you have handy and what's fresh. It's the way I actually eat BBQ at home. I will throw a steak or some ribs on and when they're cooked and waiting to be sliced, I switch to a direct heat on the BBQ and throw on what I have picked up from the shops. Any vegetables can be grilled – the great thing about them is that, unlike meat, you can burn them and they get better rather than worse. The bitter char touches enhance the flavour rather than overpower it – within reason though. Turning vegetables into charcoal is not the point and overcooked is overcooked.

Vegetables such as leeks, onions and fennel have layers. You can either slice these veg and grill them, or cook whole until black on the outside, then peel off the charred layer to reveal a cooked smoky interior. You can do the same thing with whole aubergines, blackening the skin and then peeling it off. You could even cook any of these vegetables directly on the coals for a more intense smoky effect.

All you then need is a nice dressing, some salt, maybe a few herbs and perhaps some crunchy additions. Have fun and don't discount anything as a potential ingredient. The suggestions opposite are for a spring grilled salad. (Recipe photography over the page.)

2 fennel bulbs, one left
    whole and the other
    thinly sliced
3 courgettes, thickly sliced
    lengthways
2 Tropea onions or red
    onions, cut in half
    lengthways (unpeeled)
3 spring onions
1 leek
4 white/purple/green
    sprouting broccoli stalks
3 English asparagus spears
1 globe artichoke, trimmed,
    quartered lengthways
1 small bunch dandelion
    leaves
1 romaine lettuce, cut in
    half lengthways through
    the core

FOR THE DRESSING
Olive oil, to taste
Lemon juice, to taste
4 tablespoons chopped
    flat-leaf parsley
1 small handful chives, cut
    into 2.5cm lengths
2 tablespoons puffed wild
    rice (deep-fry raw wild
    rice for a few seconds in
    180°C oil, then drain)
1 tablespoon crispy garlic
    slices (see Warm Thai
    Salad, pages 244–245)
Couple of grates of
    Parmesan cheese
Maldon salt

Cook the whole fennel bulb in the hot coals for 10 minutes until blackened, then peel off the outer charred layer. Set aside.

Lay the fennel and courgette slices, the onion halves, spring onions, leek, broccoli, asparagus and artichoke quarters on the BBQ grill. Cook, turning as needed, until the vegetables are tender and heavily charred. As they are cooked, remove them from the grill. Leave the leek until it is blackened all over, then remove and peel off the outer layer. Roughly chop up all the veg, including the whole fennel bulb.

Grill the dandelion leaves for a few seconds, and the lettuce halves on one side until almost black.

Combine all the grilled vegetables on a large platter. Dress with olive oil, lemon juice and salt, then sprinkle with the herbs, puffed wild rice, crispy garlic and Parmesan. Serve immediately.

Coal-baked aubergine salad

SERVES 6 - 8

5 aubergines
15 cherry tomatoes
50ml olive oil
3 garlic cloves, crushed
2 thyme sprigs
1 teaspoon tahini
1 tablespoon soured cream
Juice of 1 lemon
1 red onion, finely sliced
1 preserved lemon,
    chopped
2 tablespoons chopped
    mint
3 tablespoons chopped
    flat-leaf parsley
Grated zest of 2 oranges
Maldon salt and cracked
    black pepper

Get your BBQ going and set the oven to 160°C.

Prick the aubergines all over with a knife to prevent them from exploding (it happens, believe me). When the coals in your BBQ stop flaming, place the aubergines directly in them. Turn after 15 minutes and continue cooking until soft. Remove the aubergines, slice in half and scoop out the inside flesh (discard the skin). Reserve the flesh.

Whilst the aubergines are cooking in the coals, put the tomatoes in a small roasting tray with the olive oil, garlic and thyme and cook in the oven until softened. When you remove them, crush the tomatoes gently.

Mix together the tahini, soured cream and lemon juice in a large bowl to make a sauce. Add the aubergine flesh, onion, preserved lemon, mint, parsley and orange zest.

Use a slotted spoon to add the tomatoes to the bowl. Then drip in the tomato oil from the tray (discard the thyme stalks) and stir gently until you have a smooth consistency – being a little oily is fine. Season it up, then serve with fresh flatbread and lots of pulled (or 'broken') meat.

Fresh apple kimchi

SERVES 6 - 8

Not all kimchi needs time to ferment. For this simple, quick side, you need the best apples you can lay your hands on. You could also use pears. It has an amazing sweet, refreshing and spicy profile that complements pulled (or 'broken') pork better than anything I know.

4 top-quality eating/
    dessert apples
1 tablespoon kimchi paste
    (see Kimchi Hollandaise,
    page 57), or to taste
Black sesame seeds, to
    garnish (optional)

Core and slice the apples into small matchsticks (leave the skin on). Mix in a bowl with the paste, as evenly as possible without breaking the apple, but going heavy on the amount of paste. Serve immediately or very soon after. Garnish with black sesame seeds, if you like.

Korean slaw

SERVES 2 - 4

1 fennel bulb, finely sliced

1 celery stick, sliced into rounds

1 red onion, sliced

1 baby Gem lettuce, thickly sliced lengthways

1 eating/dessert apple, cored and cut into small cubes

2 tablespoons kimchi paste (see Kimchi Hollandaise, page 57)

1 spring onion, finely sliced

2 teaspoons black sesame seeds

Maldon salt and pepper

Mix everything, except the spring onion and sesame seeds, together in a bowl. Season and transfer to a serving bowl. Garnish with the seeds and spring onion and serve.

Vinegar slaw

SERVES 4 - 6

1 small white cabbage,
  thinly sliced
1 small red cabbage, thinly
  sliced
1 fennel bulb, thinly sliced
1 red onion, thinly sliced
1 tablespoon chopped
  coriander
½ tablespoon chopped
  mint
Maldon salt and cracked
  black pepper

FOR THE DRESSING
300ml cider vinegar
300g light soft brown sugar
½ teaspoon black
  peppercorns
1 teaspoon ground
  turmeric
½ teaspoon caraway seeds
1 teaspoon fennel seeds
1 teaspoon white mustard
  seeds

For the dressing, gently heat the vinegar and sugar
with the spices until it gets to 60°C. Cover the pan with
clingfilm or a tight-fitting lid and leave to cool.

Mix the cabbages, fennel and onion with a little sea salt
in a bowl. Leave for 20 minutes to soften.

Strain the vinegar and add just enough to the cabbage
mix to soak through and moisten. Mix in the herbs and
season to taste. Serve chilled or at room temperature.

Bread and butter pickles

SERVES 15

5 cucumbers (unpeeled)
2 onions, sliced
Maldon salt

FOR THE PICKLING LIQUOR
260ml cider vinegar
160g light soft brown sugar
1 teaspoon ground
    turmeric
½ teaspoon caraway seeds
1 teaspoon fennel seeds
5 black peppercorns
½ teaspoon mustard seeds

Slice the cucumbers into 2cm rounds. Place in a colander, add some fine salt to cover and mix it through with your hands. Put the colander in the sink. Set a plate on top of the cucumbers, then weigh this down with a bowl filled with water or something else that's heavy. Leave for 4 hours.

Remove the weight and plate. Turn on the cold tap and rinse the salt off the cucumbers. Drain well.

Tip the cucumbers into a pan and add the onions along with all the ingredients for the pickling liquor. Bring to the boil, then cook until the cucumbers are soft and have turned a light brown. Remove from the heat and leave to cool.

If you pack the vegetables and pickling liquor into a sterilised jar, you can store them for months in a cool, dark place. Otherwise, keep in the fridge.

Keep the liquor and use it for your Pickle Backs (a shot of bourbon followed by a shot of pickle brine).

Burnt mixed pickles

FOR THE PICKLING LIQUOR
250ml white wine vinegar
500g caster sugar
250ml water
1 bay leaf (break the leaf
   to release more flavour)
½ teaspoon caraway seeds
½ teaspoon coriander seeds
½ teaspoon black
   peppercorns

FOR THE VEGETABLES
1 cauliflower, leaves
   removed, quartered
   through the core
2 red onions, cut in half
   (unpeeled)
8 baby carrots, halved
   lengthways
6 garlic cloves, peeled
2 fresh green chillies, sliced

Get your BBQ ready for a direct grill – you want it to be hot enough to colour the veg. Mix the pickling liquor ingredients together in a pan and bring to the boil, stirring to dissolve the sugar, then leave to cool to about 60°C.

Meanwhile, put the cauliflower quarters on the grill and char the outside to a nice caramel brown colour. Don't worry about cooking them through. Pick off the outer florets and reserve (discard the central stalks/cores).

Lay the onion halves on the grill, cut side down, and blacken. Do not turn them or cook through. Remove the skin, then slice each of the halves in half and separate the 'petals'.

Combine the grilled florets, onion petals, baby carrots, garlic cloves and chillies in a sterilised vinegar-proof container. Cover with the pickling liquor and leave in the fridge for at least 24 hours before serving – up to a week is better.

If you pack the vegetables and pickling liquor into a sterilised jar and seal, you can keep them for months in a cool, dark place. Mine never last that long, so I just keep them in the fridge.

GLOSSARY

Unusual ingredients

BOQUERONES: Spanish marinated anchovy fillets

CALÇOTS: mild variety of spring onion from Catalonia

DOENJANG: Korean fermented soya bean paste

GOCHUGARU: Korean hot chilli flakes/powder

GOCHUJANG: Korean hot chilli paste

MEZCAL: Mexican spirit made from an agave plant

'NDUJA: spicy Italian sausage with a spreadable consistency

SALTED SHRIMPS: tiny shrimps fermented with salt, much used in Korean cookery

SRIRACHA: hot chilli sauce

TROPEA ONIONS: variety of red onion grown in southern Italy

Cookery terms

CARTOUCHE: a piece of greaseproof paper or baking parchment laid on top of liquid (such as in a braise) to reduce evaporation. To make one, cut the paper to the size of the container, like a lid. The cartouche doesn't have to be neat or to fit exactly, but it shouldn't leave huge gaps.

DEGLAZE: to add liquid to the pan in which meat has been cooked, to mix in and dissolve the browned meat juices and deposits from the bottom of the pan

JULIENNE: food cut into long, thin strips

REDUCE: to thicken a liquid and intensify its flavour through evaporation by boiling or simmering

UMAMI: one of the five basic tastes (after salt, sweet, sour and bitter), pleasantly savoury

INDEX

Acknowledgements

I'd like to say that I did this all by myself and let you use this space to draw pictures, write your shopping list or play hangman with a friend. However, my publisher didn't think that would be a useful use of space, and I would be lying anyway. I had lots of help and I have too many people to thank. If I've forgotten someone, I'm either truly sorry and I'll make it up to you or we're not really that close and this is the best way I could think of telling you.

Firstly, I'd like to thank the chefs I've worked under: Eric Guignard from The French Table who let me loose in his kitchen with zero experience; Nuno Mendes who let me fumble about and almost burn his house down at his Loft Supper Club; Micheal Wignall from The Latymer who taught me to shut the hell up, get my head down and get on with it; Matt Christmas from Chez Bruce for teaching me a lesson in how not to nurture talent; Adam Grey from Rhodes 24 who pushed me to finally work a stove properly and, last but not least, Adam Perry Lang who saw some talent in me and pushed me in this direction. Thanks to Tante Marie Cooking School for teaching me how to cook lots of stuff I'd never have learned to do in kitchens. I may never own a cake company but I'm sure we can all agree my frog cake was the best you've ever seen.

I'd also like to thank the brave restaurants that have hired me to run their kitchens. Tom, Jamie, Simon and Richard from Pitt Cue, Jon Carter from 580 and Scott, Maria and Simon from Noble Inns. It's been a blast and without you I'd be just some guy with a few knives and recipes.

Thanks to my suppliers over the years, Charles from Taste Tradition; Nigel from Barlochan Highlanders; Matt of The Cornish Grill; Ian of Philip Warren Butchers; Richard from Fish For Thought; Franco from Natoora; Dave from Big Green Egg; and most of all Richard and James from Turner and George (www.turnerandgeorge.co.uk) who supplied the excellent meat for this book and have done countless other generous things for me over the years. That said Richard still owes me a bottle of Pappy Van Winkle, which loses him a few friend points.

To my family: my mum, dad, brother David, Fraz, Pat, Stroma, Callum, Frank, your thousands of kids, and everyone else, and to close friends Caroline, Jim, Dan, Linz, Dave, Lee,

Tim, Gizzi, Nick, Chriss (who kept me going throughout this process), Shula (who put up with my crap whilst doing this book) and everyone else that I don't hate. Thanks for being there. Special thanks to my ex-wife Helen – without your support I probably wouldn't have had the balls to do this as a career.

To my chefs David, Luke, Liz, George, Vlad, Claire and all the rest, you're the best. Thanks for making me look good.

Thanks to Adam and Fay for saying kind words in the foreword, to Laura my publisher, to Borra my agent and her team who put up with all my shit, and thanks to Paul for the killer photography.

Most of my thanks should go to all the restaurants I've eaten in, chefs I've admired and, of course, to London itself. I get very little time to travel and without London's multicultural and inspirational restaurant scene my cooking, and most of the food in London, would be dull and lifeless. Immigration plays a huge part in my life and my success and it is the backbone of our restaurant industry. Long may it continue to enrich our lives. And thanks to anyone who has supported me or said anything nice about me ever.

Neil x

10 9 8 7 6 5 4 3 2 1

Ebury Press, an imprint of Ebury Publishing,

20 Vauxhall Bridge Road,
London, SW1V 2SA

Ebury Press is part of the Penguin Random House group
of companies whose addresses can be found at global.
penguinrandomhouse.com

Penguin
Random House
UK

First published by Ebury Press in 2016

www.eburypublishing.co.uk

A CIP catalogue record for this book is available from the British
Library

Design: Two Associates

ISBN: 9781785030871

Colour origination by Altaimage, London
Printed and bound in China by C&C Offset Printing Co., Ltd

Penguin Random House is committed to a sustainable future for
our business, our readers and our planet. This book is made from
Forest Stewardship Council® certified paper.